RESONANCE
The New Chemistry of Love

RESONANCE

The New Chemistry of Love

····

Creating a Relationship That Gives You the Intimacy AND Independence You've Always Wanted

Barbara Miller Fishman, Ph.D.,
with Laurie Ashner

HarperSanFrancisco
A Division of HarperCollins*Publishers*

Permissions acknowledgments are on p. 267.

FIRST EDITION

Library of Congress Cataloging-in-Publication Data:
Fishman, Barbara.
Resonance—the new chemistry of love : creating a relationship that gives you the intimacy and independence you've always wanted / Barbara Fishman and Laurie Ashner. — 1st ed.
p. cm.
Includes bibliographical references and index.
ISBN 0–06–250719–2 (cloth : alk. paper) —
ISBN 0–06–250720–6 (pbk. : alk. paper)
1. Marriage. 2. Interpersonal relations. 3. Intimacy (Psychology) I. Ashner, Laurie. II. Title.
HQ734.F487 1994
306.7—dc20 93–37346
CIP

94 95 96 97 98 ❖ RRD(H) 10 9 8 7 6 5 4 3 2 1

This edition is printed on acid-free paper that meets the American National Standards Institute Z39.48 Standard.

Resonance—The New Chemistry of Love
is the child of countless conversations
between Bob and me, the result of an
intellectual and loving partnership
that has delighted us during the
thirty-seven years of
our relationship.

Contents

Personal Note

The roots of this book go back to a time when I was sixteen. I was sitting in my bedroom with the door closed against the sight of my parents fighting, unable to shut out the sound of their hatred. There was nothing special about the one argument that stays in my memory, except that I was aware of my chest becoming ever tighter as their argument grew to a crescendo of spiteful accusations. I remember waiting for my mother to use her most deadly weapon—she held back until my father sounded tired and almost vulnerable, and then she let herself explode.

"I wish you were dead," she yelled. "Just you wait and see, I'll outlive you yet! One day I'll finally be free of you and your mother, and then I'll do exactly what I want."

My father's reply came slowly and without much heart, "Go to hell." It was a salvo designed to cover his retreat as he climbed the stairs to the apartment above, where his mother was waiting to greet him with an adoring embrace and an offer of food.

In those early years I wanted to protect my father from my mother's hateful words. Later I began to understand my mother's pain—she was living with a man who was never able to welcome her as a full human being with separate needs of her own into his life. She was there to be a clone of his mother.

Still later, I understood that my parents created their unhappiness together. Neither one ever gave each other the tender loving care they secretly craved. Nor was there anyone around to help. I certainly couldn't.

When I met Bob just a few years later, he too was reeling from the misery in his family. Neither of us could bear the possibility of reenacting our parent's pain, so we committed ourselves, I should say demanded of ourselves, that we do better in our own lifetimes. Perhaps because we couldn't help ourselves or our parents in those early families, we also wanted to help others.

Given this challenge, we became psychotherapists. The benefit of this remarkable work is that in order to help others, we had to explore ourselves and our own relationship. Over the years we have struggled with many of the life issues portrayed in this book—and always we have asked, How can we, or the couples we work with, do well enough to thrive?

Bob and I have found resonance many times, lost it, and found it again. That's the nature of this kind of search. But now we know more about avoiding the snares that can hold us back, and we have access to tools that help us shape and reshape a relationship so that it continues to invite resonance.

This book is a result of what we have learned so far about unions that are intentionally designed to enhance each partner. Enjoy.

Barbara Miller Fishman
January 1994

The stories in this book are based on the experiences of actual people, but the names and circumstances have been altered to ensure confidentiality.

Introduction

Chances are that at some time in your life you have experienced the power of a profoundly intimate connection with another person. Maybe you thought of it as chemistry. Or you called it passion. Whatever term you used, in those moments you felt more intimately understood and more fully alive than ever before. Words will never fully explain what happened, but you will remember it for the rest of your life. It was a peak experience in love.

We were on two old bicycles riding down a country road watching a small, white, puffy cloud on the horizon when it began to race toward us, growing larger and more ominous by the moment. Suddenly that cloud opened up and the rain splashed down. We threw our bicycles to the side of the road, but with cornfields all around, there was nothing to cover us. Instinctively, we wrapped our arms around each other, turned our heads to the sky, and tasted the rain. It was like being in a warm waterfall. We laughed, and we kissed, and we felt like the only two people in the world fortunate enough to be in love on such a magnificently beautiful rainy day.

There were candles, and a cake, and eight adults with cameras elbowing each other to snap a picture of one-year-old Kristen in a new party dress, eating a chocolate cupcake. Before we knew it, Kristen was spreading whipped cream and chocolate cake all over her face and her new dress—giggling all the time. Neither my husband nor I could keep a straight face. We burst out laughing and couldn't stop until the tears came. In a moment of super-real clarity, I knew this radiant child was part of us, and that we three were part of one vast mystery. When I caught my husband's eyes, I knew he felt it too, and we were closer together than ever before.

Joe and I have been married for over thirty-five years, long enough to see our two children come and go, long enough to go through the ups and downs of a marriage. Yet we still have moments so unforgettable that I really can't explain them. Not too long ago we were out walking on one of those rare days when spring has finally come, with a sky so blue and the air so clear that even our bodies felt new. Sitting under a flowering cherry tree, we were possessed by its sweet perfume and the rain of petals in shades of pink and red settling on us. For a moment the life force of that tree coursed through us, too. We were in touch with the miracle of life, and the miracle of a love that had sustained us for so long.

I've spent more than thirty years as a therapist studying these powerful, intimate experiences. They are moments of bonding that people feel in their bodies and know with their minds. They clarify, give insight, and deepen a relationship. I have also learned that some people never have them:

I love Nancy, but I was never "in love" with her. We get along fine, but it's never been great. Maybe I married her for the wrong reason. I thought she'd add some stability to my life. I get down even thinking about it. Sometimes I wonder if something is wrong with me. I've never been able to be passionately, irrevocably in love. You know what I mean—the kind of love to which you give yourself totally. Do you know how painful that is?

Some people are afraid of these peak experiences of love:

I can't afford a relationship right now. Relationships take you away from yourself and your goals. You risk waking up a year later with no one to have dinner with, and a career that is going downhill fast. I've paid more for those minutes of being crazy in love than I've gotten out of them.

Some couples are confused by them:

I know I can have that special feeling with other women, but I can't have it with my wife. There are days when we totally irritate each other: I can't stand the way she takes twenty minutes to order in a restaurant, and she goes crazy because I leave my shaving cream out on the sink. There are other days when we totally ignore each other. If only I could be "in love" with the woman I'm living with.

Some people have the experience, but can't recapture it:

If you ask me, the first three months of a new relationship are great, then everything goes downhill. I used to race to the door when I heard his key in the lock; now my heart sinks.

Some people would give anything to feel that kind of thrill:

In the summer it hurts the worst. I'll be running on the beach and see couples playing in the water, holding hands, kissing. It depresses me. There's not much I wouldn't give up to have a relationship that really works.

What intrigued me most was finding couples who continue to have these peak experiences throughout their lives. I have found people who still feel like lovers after three children and twenty years of marriage. How do they keep the music playing? How do they love each other without losing themselves? What do they know that the rest of us should know?

As I continued to study these couples, I began to call these peak loving experiences *resonance*. And I learned that couples who have found resonance don't have perfect relationships. They argue. Sometimes they hurt each other. They get entangled in the problems that snare most people at one time or another, but they then go on to patiently disentangle them.

"Resonant" partners are like you and me. They come to their relationships with the same types of personal problems, but the difference is that they feel safe enough to work on them and to stretch beyond them. They aren't living happily-ever-after fantasies. Every moment they share isn't an explosion of insatiable passion and incredible sex—although they do have those moments. What they experience together goes deeper than the momentary thrill of arousing or being aroused. Their relationships are passionate, and they go beyond passion.

What they have created together is a special kind of union, one in which letting go and feeling safe are possible. Anger doesn't feel too dangerous to express, and power is shared. They avoid either/or thinking (either you're right or I'm right) and instead use both/and thinking (both you and I are each somewhat right). Since they feel free to be themselves and safe enough to be together, they are more likely to encounter the peak experiences of resonance.

Many couples have the potential for resonance. To achieve it, you don't have to change your entire personality—or your partner's, for that matter. Everything you need is already inside both of you. But you need the courage to look deeply into yourself and your partner, the determination to manage any fear that might stand in the way, and a resonant vision to guide you. With a resonant relationship in place, peak experiences like the ones described at the beginning of this chapter come frequently throughout life.

To grasp what the resonant relationship is about, and the peak experiences it fosters, imagine that you're a musician who has spent long years perfecting your art. Right now you're playing a piece of jazz with your lover, who is also a musician. It's a melody you both enjoy. As you finish your solo on the piano, your partner picks up the beat, at first echoing your work and then expressing his or her own sense of the melody. You become inspired by the silvery sound, so when your turn comes again you respond with another rendition of the melody that includes the best of both of you.

On and on you both go, enjoying each other as you search for still other musical heights. In the flow, you enhance your partner and your partner enhances you.

You find that making music together is both easier and more complicated than making it alone. At times you're surprised to realize how differently you each respond to the melody. Sometimes conflict emerges and that makes the music discordant or even strident.

But there are also those exquisite moments (sometimes they feel like hours or days) when it seems as though there are invisible fibers stretched between you both, transmitting a whole range of subtle sounds that you've never been able to communicate before. You understand that you have great power to affect the other, and you learn to manage that power with love. Neither of you resists giving or receiving. Meanwhile, you're giving birth to a new musical experience—an experience of union that enhances you both. These are times neither of you will ever forget.

When two people are in resonance, each has a sense of an inner self and a clear and separate voice. Personal freedom is treasured; it's fun. Each person is also aware that he or she is part of a union—a whole that is larger than both of them together. That union has a special personality with a tempo that sometimes feels like a heartbeat. During peak experiences of love it can almost feel alive.

In this book, I'll be describing the kind of union that leads to those special resonant moments. This vision has grown out of experiences in my own life and experiences with people I've worked with in therapy. However, I did not invent resonance. Couples have enjoyed it throughout history, though they didn't call it by the same name. Love stories have been sung through time, revealing that regardless of troubled circumstances or inner problems, people find their moments of transcendence. Pure joy may quickly disappear, often it can be crushed, but authors have always tried to catch and savor it.

Tristram and Isolde's story, for instance, goes back to the Middle Ages. Tristram is a distinguished knight who falls in love with the woman betrothed to his king. Under the spell of a magic potion, these two lovers know the peak moments of love that make their devotion to each other more important than anything else in the world. As we read, we can't help hoping that their flame will survive the anger of a king, but theirs is an illicit love. And so it ends in death.

The setting is Verona during the fifteenth century. Romeo and Juliet vow their eternal love, even though their families are bitter enemies. We resonate to the magic of their passion, knowing it as a potential within us. And we feel the sense of loss, of despair, when their love also ends in death.

In the seventeenth century, the story of a love found and lost turns inward. Our hero, Cyrano de Bergerac, is a French soldier who falls in love with the beautiful Roxane. But his unsightly (to him, repulsive) nose leads him to hide that love. A fellow soldier begins to court Roxane, and Cyrano, who is a gifted poet, ghost-writes his love letters while the two men are away from home fighting the Spanish. It's through those letters that Cyrano finds a way to express the wonder of his feelings—and Roxane responds to the man who wrote them. They know resonance through the vehicle of the written word. We feel badly for poor Cyrano when he actually helps bring about the marriage of the woman he loves to another man. It's not until Cyrano is about to die that he admits to Roxane that he is the author of those beautiful letters. This is another ill-fated love, but this time because the suitor believes he's inadequate.

Even Scarlett O'Hara's love is not to be—but now it's the woman's failing. Scarlett can't love. The belle of a Southern plantation, she uses men and tosses them away. All except Ashley, whom she continues to pine for even though he's married. Meanwhile our hero, Rhett Butler, is intrigued, impassioned by Scarlett. He waits while she goes through two husbands, and finally he becomes number three. Scarlett does respond to Rhett, and they do have their very brief moments of resonance—moments we in the film audience will always remember—but this is a union that can't continue. It's too late. Their timing is off. They're out of sync.

None of these couples had a resonant vision to sustain them. They lived in times that only allowed for brief moments of passion. Perhaps because love has the power to destroy traditional social forms, it had to be seen as rare, and nearly impossible to sustain. Passionate love came to mean defiance, suffering, and even heresy rather than involvement in life, a sense of well-being, and being the best that we each can be.

However, despite frequent difficulties, resonance lives as a potential within us all. If we tend to the interior world of our hearts and the interpersonal world of our relationships, resonance will occur. Since others may be unbelieving and sometimes even hostile toward it, keeping resonance alive takes a certain vision, a certain insistent belief in our human potential. Living the resonant vision, couples will have the peak experiences of love throughout their lives.

We all come to our relationships with a vision of love—thoughts and feelings, both conscious and unconscious, tell us how to relate to each other. These visions can lead to resonance, or when they inhibit a sense of safety and opportunities for change, they can lead to grief.

One very common vision leads toward what I call the *merged relationship*. In this type of relationship, togetherness becomes so important that personal freedom is neglected, and traditional gender roles prevail. While merging with a partner can lead to stable living and family life, it also can result in homes that feel more like prisons.

Others have a vision of what I call an *exchange relationship*. Couples in these types of relationships are so intent on maintaining their personal freedom—their careers, separate friends, private interests—that being in a relationship becomes almost unimportant in comparison. They make sure what they give is reciprocated so that neither one invests more than the other. This can become a careful, guarded, insecure love. When the exchange becomes extreme, unions receive so little attention that they're very likely to die without either partner ever experiencing intimacy.

In this book, I'll help you learn to recognize the signs of a merged and an exchange relationship, why we tend to create them, and what it is about each type of relationship that stands in the way of resonance. There are choices to be made in relationships, forks in the road that lead toward very different end points. You'll see those junctions more clearly so that it will be less likely that you'll arrive at a relationship without at least knowing how you got there.

You'll also understand:

• Why too much closeness in a relationship is just as damaging as too much freedom.

• How to balance intimacy with autonomy by learning to follow your own path while still feeling rooted in a relationship.

• How to enhance your relationship by freeing yourself of standard notions of what it means to be a "real man" or a "real woman."

• How to stop allowing your partners to control you, and how to avoid the pitfalls of trying to control them.

• How to use your anger to explore yourself instead of turning it into the hostility that's destructive to relationships.

• How to increase your awareness by accessing your "felt sense."

• How to use the process of "double vision" to understand your partner without losing your sense of self.

• How money can be used to create opportunities for resonance.

• How to use the tools of resonance to set the stage for peak sexual experiences.

I bring you my experience as a gift with the hope that it will be helpful, not as a simple answer to the difficulties involved in coupling but as a series of insights that can both illuminate your own relationships and help you as an individual be the best that you can be.

CHAPTER I

Visions of Love

> We are not separated from other(s) . . . by a
> boundary, but simply by another mode of vision.
> —Herman Hesse, *Demian*

Over the past thirty years I've worked with hundreds of couples who have come into therapy because their relationships were in trouble. Whether they were aware of it or not, each of these people had a vision of love—thoughts, feelings, and dreams about how relationships work. When things went wrong they blamed themselves or their partners, but often the trouble was with their visions.

You have a vision of love, whether you fully understand it or not. And I'm going to suggest that while you may not have the type of relationship you want right now, you have what you've envisioned—not what your first romantic dreams led you to expect, but the fruit or the yield of those dreams—and you can envision something else.

What Do You Expect from Love?

From the very first moment we meet someone, we count on our personal vision of love to guide us in starting a relationship. That means we don't even have to think about a whole range of questions—Who calls for a date? Who pays for dinner?—because our vision most often provides the answers.

When we fall in love, we create a shared vision of a relationship—some mixture of our own and our partner's original versions. We spend countless hours getting to know each other, telling stories and sharing personal secrets, shaping and reshaping our thoughts about love.

If the effort is successful, we begin to feel that our relationship is a good "fit." If the effort is unsuccessful and our visions clash, we begin to think that no matter how terrific the other person might be, he or she just isn't right.

Sometimes a couple's visions of love are too different.

> The other night when I came home, I tried to kiss her, and all I got was a gruff: "Make the salad. I'm late for an evening meeting." I like spending time together, but all she cares about is her career.

Sometimes we try too hard to make our relationship conform to one vision. Perhaps it's the one extolled by today's generation—the new way, the modern way to love.

> We're each separate individuals. I wouldn't dream of changing my name or giving up my bank account. It simply wouldn't work.

Sometimes we instinctively adopt our parent's vision of a relationship.

> I know we're not happy together, but I keep thinking that's the way my parents did it, and it worked for them! Certain things don't change. Besides, I don't really know any other way to love.

A particular vision can work well at one point but not later on. For example, the dream of an equal relationship with enough "space" for each person to follow his or her different path can fall apart when a baby arrives.

> We both used to lead fairly independent lives, with two high-powered jobs. But since the baby came I've cut back my hours. I'm stuck inside the house while he still spends three nights a week out with his friends.

Or, the original vision may have included lots of closeness, and this may become overwhelming to one person.

> We used to do everything together until he started to pull away. I don't understand what's happening.

The truth is, we all have our expectations of relationships, but some visions are more flexible, more supple—they change as we ourselves change. They offer greater potential for both personal freedom and intimacy. That's the kind of vision that leads to resonance.

Where Did You Learn About Love?

Where does your particular vision of love come from?

Your parents provided your first lesson in love and marriage. It's probably your model for how two people talk to each other, how they fight, whether they touch, and if relationships can be happy. Because this was a firsthand experience, it was bound to make its mark, whether or not the relationship worked.

Amy, twenty-eight, discovered this after a particularly upsetting argument with her husband.

She said, "When I could finally get him to talk about what was wrong, he said I smothered him—that I wanted so much attention he never had room to breathe. I stood there, feeling like I was going to scream—he was so insensitive—and suddenly I thought back twenty years, to when I was ten years old. I could hear my parents fighting, using almost the same words. We were fighting in just the same way. I went out of my way to marry a man I thought was nothing like my father, and still, I ended up feeling like my mother!"

Amy thought she had a different kind of relationship than her mother had, but her vision of how to manage conflict in a relationship was almost exactly the same as her mother's, and so was the fallout.

But it's not only family that influences our visions of love; our friends do also. We see what they do; we borrow their solutions and try them out on our own relationships.

A woman may ask, "I would love it if you were more affectionate with me, even if we're with other people. Michael kisses his girlfriend in public; why can't you?"

To which the man may say, "If you knew how much Michael is affectionate with other women, you wouldn't think he's such a nice guy!"

The media also has an enormous influence on the way we think about our relationships. Images of stilted, dishonest communication on daytime soaps show family lives where loving is impossible. Evening television, ostensibly about more ordinary people, is often filled with stereotyped images of men and women and recurrent abuse.

Action dramas are even less helpful—the frequency with which people resort to bombs and guns, the ease of killing, the speed with which wounds heal, and the avoidance of psychic pain are all facets of a cultural saga built on a denial of our human vulnerability. And an awareness of our own and our partner's vulnerability is basic to good loving.

There is still another kind of influence on our visions of love: Each era has its own biases, its own prescriptions for the good life, and each generation its own challenges.

The vision of a house with a white picket fence, suggesting security, privacy, and containment, met the needs of society in the 1950s. The image of the dual-career couple, each with briefcase in hand, met the individualistic needs of people in the 1980s. We are creatures of our times.

Sometimes we find people in the world around us who work well together—some parents know how to manage conflict, model warmth and caring, and respect each other's separate interests. There are people in every generation who do the same. Even so, we have to tailor-make our own vision so that it works for us. No one else's vision can do that. There are many influences on the way we love; we take them in, and they become part of us. But that doesn't mean we can't separate from them enough to envision something else.

What You Envision Shapes the Way You Love

The institution of marriage may seem already there, likes bricks and mortar, and all we have to do is fit into it. Many people think this way, and it allows them very little freedom to shape their own relationships. But loving isn't just an automatic or inherited response, we learn it.

Lots of human energy is burned keeping old customs going; in fact, we re-create those customs every day! It takes the work of every generation, and many human beings, to keep the institution of marriage functioning as it is. We learn how to be close and how to argue by watching others, and then we hone those skills every day in our relationships. Even the words we use support what has been done before: Love is often described in terms of ownership; marriage implies sleeping together every night.

Yet there are couples who strike out in a different direction. They shape the way they love to fit their current needs—and so create a relationship that's tailor-made. Their minds and hearts are flexible as they envision the kind of relationship they want to live within.

You can do this, too. But first you need to pay attention to the relationship vision you currently have. Often it can be a patchwork of contradictions, many of which are subconscious.

Bringing your relationship vision into awareness is essential for three reasons: First, you can only create a relationship according to the vision of love you actually hold. For example, if you want more closeness, and your vision doesn't include a way of expressing anger, your anger will get in the way of the very closeness you want. One man became aware of this part of his vision. As he faced the challenge of changing it, he found that he had to begin feeling his anger: "I can't believe how numb I was all those years. Sure we spend more time fighting now, but I'm involved. I care. When the sparks fly we actually feel closer!"

Your vision of love is shaping the future of your relationship, and you may not even know how. If you believe, for instance, that, whoever your lover is, he or she will always end up leaving you, it's likely you'll play a part in making that come true. One woman in therapy is convinced that her husband will eventually leave because "that's what men do." Too proud to admit she's afraid, she covers her fear with anger: "He's never there when I need him. He doesn't compliment me enough. Besides, he's too fat." Without awareness, this woman is making her fear become a reality by driving her husband away.

Also, if you feel something is missing in your relationship, you have no hope of changing it unless you know how your vision interferes. A creative businessman in therapy, who thrives on the give and take of team effort at work, finds that at home he's often irritable and bored, and he dreams of having a more exciting relationship. Unfortunately, he believes that work and home should be kept separate. His vision of love helps keep his family life dull by keeping him from talking about his work, with all the excitement and energy it carries for him.

Finally, some visions spell trouble from the start. One woman believes that her poor self-esteem will disappear once she's in a relationship. That belief is a problem in itself. No single person can be the solution to another person's internal problems. Even to attempt to solve one's problems that way causes trouble.

When I begin talking about how visions influence our relationships, and how we have created what we envisioned, someone usually argues, "I didn't envision a husband who would abuse me." Or, "Why would I ever want another rendition of my mother?"

The woman who married an abusing man didn't wish for that; nevertheless, her vision of love contained the potential for abuse, and without awareness she and her husband found themselves creating the kind of relationship that fosters it. For instance, when they argued they followed an unspoken rule prescribing a fight to the bitter end, and that often led to her unconditional surrender.

You can explore your vision of love, discover who and what influenced it, and how it came into being. This is a personal journey that will give you the freedom to select and innovate, to taste and repudiate, until you create a vision that truly feels authentic and moves you toward resonance.

How to Explore Your Vision of Love

What do you mean when you say you're in love? To explore the vision that guides your relationship, take a few moments to think about each of the following topics.

How do you picture your personal relationship?

Are the two of you close and loving? Are you living separate lives? Are you really at war?

A man recently told me that he felt secure living a married life. A home and two children felt like success.

A woman said, "I love our life together. We each like our work. I spend free time with my good friends; he likes to play ball with his. It couldn't be better."

Should you and your partner become mom and dad in a traditional style of family life? Should you be equals? Financially? Emotionally? Educationally?

Should you maintain the romance even if you've been married for many years?

How do you expect a relationship to change your life?

The rules we believe are necessary for a relationship go deeper than the marital vow that we remain true "until death do you part." Many of us follow other, more subtle rules, such as, I can't have female friends once I marry her. I shouldn't want to vacation alone. I can't stay home when he visits his parents. It's wrong to have fantasies about being with someone else. And so on.

What subtle rules do you have about love, friendships, vacations, home, or fantasy life?

Cynthia and Joseph follow unspoken rules that cause trouble. The only time he touches her, it's a signal that he wants sex. In response, Cynthia follows an unspoken rule of her own—avoid his touch.

Martha and Bernard have another kind of rule. Every five or six weeks, they get a baby-sitter and go off to a local motel for good sex, rest, and relaxation. That works well for them.

What do you expect from someone who loves you?

From your partner, do you expect affection . . . friendship . . . to make love more or less often . . . to be treated with respect?

What is your idea of a woman's role in a relationship? A man's? Do wives do the shopping and men take out the garbage? Do women work, take care of babies, and manage the household while men make the "real money"?

Henry's response to this question was to quickly say that he wanted a wife, a homemaker, and a mother of his children.

Geraldine's vision was of a man who would be a partner, a friend, and a travel companion.

Don't think about what's right or even what makes sense. Think about what leads to your personal well-being.

What do you really want from a loving relationship?

Your personal expectations include everything you believe about intimate relationships, from "A relationship will solve all my problems" to "If you want security, get a German Shepherd, not a husband."

Have you ever said the following?

"Love is forever."

"It's natural for two people who have been together for years to lose interest in each other."

"If you're married, you're never lonely."

"I can't name one couple that is really happy together."

"You can't expect him to be excited like he used to be. The bloom is off the rose."

"True love heals."

If you remember repeating a rendition of any of these statements, they're part of your vision of a relationship—a set of expectations that needs to be considered and challenged, then accepted or rejected.

You may be a cynic and expect very little from love. That's what happens in this time of high divorce rates. Or perhaps you're a true romantic; you're certainly not alone if you dream of passionate love forever. Maybe you want a house surrounded by a white picket fence that protects you from the dangers of our world.

Perhaps you believe that it's possible to have a long-term relationship that goes beyond security and enhances both partners, despite the obstacles that stand in the way.

Give some thought to what you expect from a loving relationship.

Three Visions of Love

In my therapeutic work and research, I've listened closely to many people's ideas about love, and certain themes have emerged over and over again. I have identified three common relationship visions that people use to guide them: *exchange, merged,* and *resonant.*

People in an exchange describe their relationship as a background to their lives. Personal interests, career, friendships come first. Separateness, freedom from traditional gender roles, and autonomy are the goals.

People in merged relationships make togetherness primary, so much so that their individual interests come second. They follow traditional gender roles. These are the couples who look for a lifestyle that offers family and security.

Those in resonance understand that both separateness and closeness are important, that gender roles can be shaped according to talent and desire. They know they need the kind of relationship that allows for both personal freedom and intimacy.

The first step toward creating a relationship that works is to understand your personal vision. In the next three chapters, I will describe these visions in depth. Chances are, one of them will come close to describing your relationship.

The quiz that follows has a dual purpose. First, it's designed to supplement your thinking about your relationship and to help you clarify your ideas. In addition, it will help you uncover which of these three common visions of love is paramount in your life and that so profoundly shapes your relationship.

What's Your Vision of Love?

1. You're taking a course at the local university, and a young woman, Cheryl, is assigned to your study group. When she misses a meeting because her three-year-old has a cold, you think:

A. What's wrong with Cheryl's husband? Why can't he wipe a runny nose when the final exam is next week?
B. It's amazing that Cheryl would even try to take a class this demanding when she has the responsibility of a baby.
C. Her child must have a bad cold or Cheryl and her husband wouldn't have decided that it was important one of them stay home.

2. The friends you each spend the most time with since you've become a couple are:

A. The people you've each known since high school and college, and your individual friends from work.
B. Other couples; people you met together and "double" with.
C. A mixture of both—you have separate friends and mutual friends.

3. You sit in front of the TV fighting over the remote control night after night. What do you finally decide?

A. One of you gets the "clicker" on Mondays, Wednesdays, and Fridays; the other gets the rest of the week, except on the seventh day the TV rests.

B. It's not your fault if your partner has no taste; if he or she doesn't like what you're watching, let him or her go to another room.

C. It's time to discuss why "control of the clicker" is an issue in your relationship and to try to make room for each person's needs.

4. What do you want most in a relationship?

A. Your freedom; you want to continue to pursue your own interests, your own friends.

B. Togetherness; you want your family to come first, friends second.

C. Creativity and spontaneity, whether with family, friends, or at work.

5. When your partner gets a raise, you feel:

A. Happy, but a little jealous.

B. Thrilled, because you need a new dining room table.

C. Content, because you're both working toward a common goal—more income.

6. You both want to make a donation to charity, but you have different causes you believe in. The way you decide to work it is:

A. You both give separately to the causes you believe in.

B. You make one joint donation to a cause you can agree on.

C. You split the total amount you can afford to give in three parts. You each end up with your own amount to donate, while the third goes to a cause you can both support.

7. You mention your plan to have dinner with a friend. You notice your lover is sulking. What do you do?

A. Try to ignore it. Your partner went out the other night, and fair is fair.

B. Feel guilty. You might even stay home because it's just not worth another fight.

C. Settle on a late night date together, after you have dinner with your friend.

8. How many savings accounts do you have?

A. Two. You keep your savings entirely separate.

B. One. Everything you earn goes in the same pot.

C. You might have one account or several accounts, but it's clear that yours is a joint enterprise and each person has a powerful voice.

9. You want to go on vacation. When you mention it to your partner, he or she says, "I want to go too, but I don't think it's realistic." What is your most likely response?

A. "Fine. Stay home if you like, but I really need to get away."

B. "That's it. I give up. You always say no to anything I want to do."

C. "If we can find a solution to whatever is bothering you, would you want to go?"

10. Your fiancé planned a ski trip long before you got engaged. The trip is designed for singles, and the enormous deposit is non-refundable. You tell your fiancé:

A. "Have fun! You can reach me at Club Med. I haven't had the pleasure of a weekend affair for a long time."

B. "If you still want to go on this trip, you aren't ready to settle down. I need a monogamous relationship."

C. "It's a bind that they won't give you a refund. I'd prefer that we plan to do something else together soon so that I don't sit home getting jealous and crazy. What do you want?"

11. Your child wakes up, covered with little red spots. Who stays home?

   A. Whoever didn't stay home the last time this happened.
   B. Mom, of course.
   C. It's not an automatic decision but something you deal
   with each time it happens.

12. You are invited to George and Lainie's home for dinner, and you discover George in the kitchen cooking. What's the first thought that comes to your mind?

   A. "Makes sense, since it's George's friends that are invited
   to dinner, not Lainie's."
   B. "I wish I had a camera. This is something you'd never see
   in my house."
   C. "George must love to cook."

13. You've agreed to split the housework fifty/fifty, now that you're both working. When there's a crisis at work, your partner asks you to help out by doing more of the housework. You think:

   A. No way. It's unfair to break your original contract and
   the very principles basic to the relationship.
   B. It was never fifty/fifty anyway; guess who was doing most
   of the work?
   C. Of course you'll help out; when circumstances change,
   your relationship changes.

14. How much freedom do you need in a relationship?

   A. You couldn't exist without your freedom.
   B. You're frightened of too much freedom. You think it
   leads to affairs and the death of the relationship.
   C. You need your freedom, but that doesn't mean you want
   to have an affair. You also need to be committed.

15. If your partner didn't want you to take a class at a local college you'd feel:

A. Outraged. Who is he or she to try to control you?
B. Angry. But it's a good bet you wouldn't end up taking the course because you wouldn't want to listen to the complaining night after night.
C. Curious. You'd want to understand why before you made any judgments.

16. When you think of Paul and Linda McCartney, Hillary and Bill Clinton, Tom Cruise and Nicole Kidman, you wonder:

A. How they divide their money.
B. How any man can allow his wife to spend so much time away from home.
C. How great it would be if you and your lover could be creative together.

17. Which statement most closely explains the reason why your last relationship didn't work out?

A. Your interests were so different that you basically just went your separate ways. Sex became rare; really good sex disappeared.
B. One of you wanted more sex than the other, so one person felt deprived and the other felt used.
C. Neither of you felt safe enough, and free enough, to be yourselves.

18. How do you two decide what time to go to bed?

A. You each go to sleep when you're sleepy, mostly at different times.
B. It's not even a question: same time, every night, together.
C. It's not carved in stone, but you enjoy the close time that happens before falling asleep.

19. Who initiates sex?

A. It's supposed to be equal.
B. It's supposed to be the man.
C. It depends on who feels turned on.

20. You want to visit your family for Thanksgiving. Your partner:

A. Doesn't enjoy your family and so decides to stay home.
B. Complains loudly, wanting to stay home so you can be together.
C. Talks to you about how you both feel about celebrating holidays, recognizing that each of you needs a relationship with family as well as a commitment to your own union.

Scoring

Give yourself five points for every A answer, three points for every B answer, and one point for every C answer.

75–100 points: Your relationship vision falls into the pattern I call "exchange." Personal freedom is very important to you. You've had a taste of relationships that were suffocating. Now you're more careful to maintain your separate space. You're committed to an "equal relationship," a careful balance of rights and responsibilities. Chapter 2 outlines the strengths of your vision of love—and its basic dilemma.

45–74 points: What you want out of a relationship is togetherness, by which you mean someone who supports and understands you. You have a vision of relationships I think of as "merged." Chapter 3 explains why this type of vision is so prevalent in our society, why it works so well when you first fall in love, and why it tends to disappoint in the long run.

Less than 44: You're on the road to resonance—the best that you and your partner can be, separate and together. Your relationship is important to you, but so is your personal growth. In a pulsating rhythm, the two of you move back and forth from your separate lives to your life together, holding on to neither. You're on a journey together, and the rest of this book can serve as a guide.

No clear answers? Some couples make use of two or even all three visions. For instance, the exchange vision might guide their financial relationship, the merged vision might shape their parenting style, and the resonant vision might guide their sexual union.

To evaluate your answers further, return to the individual items. If you tend to choose A in questions about a particular relationship arena, you are following the exchange vision. Choosing B reflects the merged vision and C the resonant vision. Use the following guide.

Relationship Arena	Questions
Power and conflict:	3,9,15,18
Gender roles:	1,11,12,13
Money and work:	5,6,8,16
Sex:	10,14,17,19
Friends, family life:	2,4,7,20

Every one of us has a vision of what it means to be in a loving relationship, even if the reality turns out to be far from happy. For some, that vision of love is a reflection of their parent's union; for others, it's the path of their generation.

But loving is a very personal act—you can only learn by doing it. At best that means being aware of your vision of loving and sharing it with the person you love. It means creating a shared vision, testing it out, thinking about what went wrong, and trying again.

Reading about the visions of others, whether they be exchange, merged, or resonant, makes it more likely that you'll be aware of the many subtle facets of your own vision. That's the first step toward creating a shared vision, and that leads to the kind of relationship that fits you both.

CHAPTER 2

The Exchange Relationship—
When You're Clearly Separate

Humans avoid costly, and seek rewarding . . .
relationships . . . to the end that their profits are
maximized and their losses are minimized.
—Ivan Nye,
"Choice, Exchange and the Family,"
Contemporary Theories About the Family

The woman who sat in front of me spoke slowly and carefully, but anger flickered in her eyes. "Everything David does irritates me these days," she said. "Little things, like leaving his towel on the floor, make me want to scream. Lately the tension is so thick you can cut it with a knife. I stay at the office until nine organizing files, writing memos, and driving my staff crazy because I don't want to go home."

She slid her bracelet back and forth, working it over the widest part of her hand. "David knows something is wrong between us, but so far I've managed to avoid a showdown. Sometimes I catch him looking at me when he doesn't think I'm paying attention. He's like a cat at a mouse hole. He wants something from me that I just can't give him right now."

Brushing away a strand of pure auburn hair that fell over her eyes, she looked at me sadly. "I care about him, I really do. But

I'm not sure I'm in love with him anymore. It's hard to believe I'm saying this, because a month ago I thought it would last forever."

A month ago, David, vice president in charge of acquisitions for a real estate firm, was traveling to three different cities a week. The woman, Robin, a lawyer associated with one of the most prestigious firms in town, often found herself on the opposite coast from him. Their private joke was that they'd moved in together to be sure of seeing each other once in a while.

"Were you ever lonely?" I asked Robin. She looked puzzled.

"Well, no. Not exactly. Something in our crazy bi-coastal relationship satisfied me," she admitted. "I never had to make excuses to him for staying late at the office or for all of the entertaining I had to do. We'd both been married before and neither of us wanted to be connected at the hip. But when we were together it was wonderful, and I was sure it was love."

Then the bottom fell out of the real estate market and David lost his job, as well as a fortune he had personally invested. Robin, shocked and sympathetic, tried to soothe him. But soon she began to feel uncomfortable around him in a way she never had before.

"My stomach was constantly in knots." she said. "I knew enough about the market to know that it could take David a year to find another position, and what he found may not come close to what he had. I kept thinking that our success story was ending in failure. We started to argue about stupid things."

She paused, thinking, then said, "I'm supporting the two of us now. I have the money to do it; none of this is about dollars and cents. But deep inside, I feel cheated. The worst thing is, no one understands how I feel. Everyone talks about how awful it is for David."

"He's really changed," she added bitterly. "Just last night he talked about running off to an island. He wants me to quit my job and open a bed and breakfast place with him. Maybe it's just a fantasy—being out of work is hard on him—but talk like that terrifies me. I loved the life we had. I never wanted it to change."

She looked at me unhappily. "Just saying these things makes me feel like some kind of a monster. I get in these black moods where I think, What's wrong with me? David really needs me now and all I can think of is how to tell him that I want out of this relationship before we really hurt each other."

Why did Robin doubt that she and David could stay together once he lost his job? After all, money wasn't a problem, and they did care about each other. What went wrong?

To answer these questions, it's important to understand how people connect in the first place. It happens nonverbally, as eyes meet and flash sexual attraction. And it happens through words, as people reveal their histories, their secrets. But what keeps people together is a shared vision of love.

Long before she met David, Robin had a vision of the type of relationship she wanted. A career, success, and lots of room for her separate life were important to her.

Robin was amazed to find that David had the same vision for himself. It seemed like a perfect match. They each had a partner devoted to making their vision real. But when he lost his job, they lost that shared vision. When he stopped striving for the same type of success, their visions clashed, and Robin began to feel that no matter how terrific he was, David was not the right person for her.

Robin's attitudes, feelings, and experience are typical of men and women who share an exchange relationship.

The "I" and "We" of Relationships

In order to understand what an exchange relationship is about, let's take a closer look at how any two lovers relate.

To begin with, we all know ourselves in two basic ways: as a distinctly separate self, or an "I," and as part of a larger union, a "we."

Eating breakfast, going to work, listening to music, I alone experience my world, according to the way I think and through my senses. "We" experiences are the interdependent times when two people understand that they require each other. When "we" are listening to music, I am not only interested in my reaction but in yours as well, and it feels good when our tastes are similar. Sharing secrets, developing a common taste in films, or enjoying a beautiful sunset together are other examples of "we" experiences.

It is important that people develop both their "I" as well as their "we." In fact, the two states are so bound together that it is probably impossible to develop either one fully without the other. After all, we wouldn't know life at all if it weren't for the "we" that occurs at conception. And a well-developed union depends on two fully participating separate selves.

For some people, experiences of either "I" or "we" are so frightening they protect themselves from fully knowing one or the other state. Others find our urban culture's focus on self is so mesmerizing they don't pay enough attention to their need for union.

In an exchange relationship, the "I" is all-important while the "we" fades into the background. Each person attends to his or her own needs, making sure the other doesn't tamper with his or her "personal space." At their best, exchange relationships allow for exciting, independent lifestyles and free and equal partners.

For me, Tom and Cherie are an example of a successful exchange. She is a successful writer, he a talented, busy actor. Their careers are the keystones of their lives; when they're busy, they're happy. When they aren't busy, they're looking for work. That's when Tom, in particular, feels frustrated that Cherie isn't more available. Fortunately, they've both been busy for the past few years.

With one apartment in New York and another in Los Angeles, they have plenty of "space" to lead their separate lives. They tell me that their relationship works because by the time they get together they really want to be. Otherwise, their telephone bills are very high. It doesn't matter, though; they both make enough money to support their lifestyle. Will this relationship last? Perhaps that's the wrong question to ask people in a modern exchange. It works for now, and that's the important thing.

The Exchange Relationship in History

Relationships in which the "I" is most important have a long tradition. The "oldest profession in the world," prostitution, is an exchange of money for sex. Courtesans sometimes exchanged sex for the power that came along with their wealthy partners.

In the past, when a lonely frontiersman answered an advertisement placed by a woman offering to sell her services in exchange for a marriage certificate, love wasn't part of the deal. Even today there are women who offer their wifely services for status and money, and men who offer their salaries for a home life.

Take Debbie and Paul, for example. Their relationship could have occurred a century ago. When I asked why, at twenty-eight, blond, blue-eyed, and beautiful Debbie was marrying a man of fifty-two, she was quick to respond.

"Paul is a real catch—millions of dollars, good looking, and he wants to give me everything I want. You have to understand, I come from a poor family, and I've been knocked around by life. Now I'm finally going to have some security. He's the answer to my dreams. Do you know he's buying me a new Jaguar? And the diamond ring we just ordered is five carats! All he asks in return is that when he has to travel—for work or pleasure—I go with him. Of course, I'll have to give up my job, but I never liked working anyway. There will be plenty for me to do. I'll spend time decorating our new house and seeing friends. I'll have fun."

It was a good deal for Paul, too. As he said, "The truth is, I don't do well living alone. I get tired of the bar scene and the late nights, and I start to drink too much. Debbie can provide me with the home base I need. But she has to understand, it will work as long as she doesn't make too many demands on my time—and as long as she doesn't want kids. I've done that trip already. I've already told her I'm too old for it."

These two offer an example of an old-style exchange, in which the woman trades her companionship and her homemaking capacity for the man's money and status. As women in our country began to work and commanded salaries of their own, another kind of exchange became possible—one based on economic equality and an avoidance of traditional gender roles. But that means that both people need to have successful careers from which they ideally earn an equal amount of money. As you'll see, these people are also fairly independent and gain substantial satisfaction from personal interests and friendships. They don't look for a lot of closeness.

But will a relationship like this satisfy? Or, will the vision lose its attraction if the woman loses her job or if the man has an affair? Their vision doesn't make room for the stress that will occur if one of them wants a child. They often have little time for their "home base." I have found that this is often a temporary arrangement.

Is Your Relationship a Modern Exchange?

Regardless of the specific details of their relationships, partners in a modern exchange share a common profile. Perhaps it also describes your relationship.

*Personal freedom is more important to you than the
experience of union with another person.*

It isn't that you don't want a relationship. You do. But you believe it is essential that both you and your lover develop your own talents and follow your own interests. That's more important than simply being in a relationship. When you say you're in love, you mean you've found someone who enhances your life but doesn't interfere with it.

Richard loves Sharon. He actually wants to live with her. She's pretty, smart, and a good lawyer. But she wants him to move from Boston to Princeton, where she's living. In his mind, that's asking too much. He argues that the move would be too disruptive to his career. On the other hand, Sharon has a thriving private practice in domestic law. She argues that it would be easier for him to change jobs than for her to start another business. But Richard isn't buying into that. If she doesn't change her mind fairly soon, he's ready to give up on the relationship.

*Your equality rests on your ability to pay your own way.
If one of you can't, there's trouble.*

Your career is important to you, and you can't feel content for long with someone who doesn't feel the same. You're not attracted to dreamers, starving artists, or people who need you to take care of them. Nor are you necessarily searching for someone wealthy. By no means do you want to be taken care of yourself. In fact, people who know you well say your problem is that you refuse to let anyone pamper you, even for a moment. You want to be valued and appreciated for who you are—but you don't want to owe anyone.

What are you looking for? A friend, an economic partner, and an equal. This means you both must be able to pay your own way.

Nancy and Rodger were getting married in a few months. He was a successful investment broker, and she was a management consultant who was usually sought after by corporations all around the country. But times were tough, and Nancy didn't have any new contracts in the pipe line.

"Rodger keeps telling me not to worry about money," she said. "Especially since I've been sending some of my clients his way, he had become pretty wealthy. But I never, ever feel like this money is ours. I am constantly worried about pulling my own weight financially, and when I don't have any consulting I start to panic. It's like he'll leave me or something if I can't keep up.

"When I drive his car, I feel like I'm driving *his* car, not *our* car. So here I am tooling around in this great, yellow-colored Porsche and not really enjoying it. It's like a mind block; rationally, I know one thing, emotionally, I feel another. I know it's about safety— and the fear of being dependent, but I can't stop feeling scared.

"And these fights always spring up: who contributed more to this or that article; who should pay the phone bill. I realize it's just me, trying to say that I contribute, but I can't help it. I see so many women who have no problem spending their husband's money and feeling that the emotional contribution they make is plenty. But I'm not one of them. I can't be like that. When I ask myself what's wrong with my kind of relationship, I guess it's that you never really feel secure."

It's extremely important to you that you're both fair,
that neither one of you is taking advantage of the other.

Celeste and Jerry have negotiated a host of agreements with each other to keep things fair: She does the meals, and he does the laundry. They've put off having children because Jerry hasn't agreed to share the parenting equally.

These two try hard to keep things even, as if there's some great scoreboard in the sky. And if the score is uneven, as it was when

Jerry was too busy to do the weekly laundry, Celeste was quick to say, "You're not holding up your end of the bargain. I can't let you take advantage of me."

Their financial arrangements are a reflection of the same theme. Each has their own separate checking account as well as a savings account. Their system to cover major expenses is logical: Since Celeste makes 60 percent of the income, she pays 60 percent of the rent. Although they don't make a big issue out of it, they know exactly who contributed every piece of furniture, artwork, or appliance in the house. They try to avoid joint ownership of things. It would be too messy if they had to separate. What's most important in a modern exchange is that neither person gives more than the other. An exchange isn't as much cold and calculating as self-protective.

It's likely that you once had a relationship—with a lover or a parent—that left you feeling suffocated.

Not surprisingly, many exchange relationships are second marriages. People who prefer the exchange frequently have been in previous relationships that allowed them little personal freedom. Some have had very difficult first marriages. They are very concerned that neither person in the new relationship loses the freedom so recently won.

If this is your first serious relationship and you opt for an exchange, chances are your parents were in a relationship riddled with traditional gender-role behavior (husbands do this; wives do that) and the conflict and jealousy this can engender. All this made their relationship feel more like a prison. Now closeness frightens you. You've decided to avoid the traditional route, knowing you couldn't live that way.

But the route you've chosen to take is challenging. While traditional roles can feel enslaving to those caught in them, there is also a source of power in them that can be hard to give up, since within each person's prescribed sphere he or she has complete authority. Shouldn't a woman tell the man how to diaper their baby? Doesn't a man have the right to manage investments? Traditional roles are a double-edged sword. Having wrestled with gender-role problems, exchange couples try to avoid being enslaved by them, and they want to function in the roles often assigned to the other gender. They want to share the burdens of a household, and they want to develop their capacity to parent as well as to make money.

Take Karen and Philip, for example. Before they met, Karen grew up in Asheville, North Carolina, and at nineteen married a boy she met in high school. They quickly had two children, so almost before she was a fully grown adult she found herself immersed in the homemaker and parenting roles. Meanwhile, her husband became an accountant, joined the local Chamber of Commerce, and spent weekends playing one or another sport, or watching others play them on television. He made the money and assumed the power to give her a weekly allowance for household expenses, which she accepted without grumbling. Her power was in the parenting role. He stayed out of the way of raising their children, bowing to her judgment most of the time.

Feeling suffocated by her life, Karen did the unthinkable. One day, after a particularly bad fight, she emptied the checking account, got into the car with the kids, and traveled to Philadelphia where her sister lived.

During the next five years Karen went through a transformation in her thinking about relationships, and by the time she met Philip she had the exchange vision clearly in mind. Now they dream of buying a house in which they will both equally invest. Certainly they will each continue to work and, just as they have for years, continue to take care of themselves.

Philip was very clear about it. "Even now, while we're living together at Karen's place, we're sharing the household tasks. To make sure there's no confusion, we keep a schedule of our separate responsibilities on the side of the refrigerator. It works better that way. Someday we'll also have a child of our own, and that will also be a joint venture."

"No way do I want to be the only one responsible for the family any more," Karen said, agreeing with Philip. "I feel lucky to have found a man who really wants to pull his own weight. But sometimes I can't believe it's true, and I get frightened about having a baby. Will you really take time off when the baby is sick?"

"I get angry when you ask such a question," Philip responded. "It makes me think you don't believe in me. Besides, I know being a mother means a lot to you, and I wonder if you'll take over before I get a chance to be a real father."

As Karen and Philip are finding, it's not easy to break out of traditional gender roles, especially when they are the only experience of a male and female relationship you've had. Yet exchange couples do break out. In the end they may make compromises, but their relationships look very different from that of their parents—or of many first marriages.

Your answer to most problems with your partner is, "Let's negotiate."

A keystone of the exchange is the desire to reason through each conflict together, instead of allowing one person to take charge. Often the process is a negotiation: "I'll do this, if you do that." This is a very important shift in the way the business of family life is accomplished. There is no tyranny here; in fact, partners are committed to a more democratic style of decision making.

However, even in an exchange, partners don't always approach conflicts rationally. People often come to relationships with a history of being dominated, and so expect it will happen again. For instance, if someone has been dominated in a previous relationship, he or she may expect to be dominated in the very next quarrel, even if that's not the other's intention. The situation gets more difficult if a person not only expects to be dominated but also feels unloved if it doesn't happen.

A man I know felt owned and dominated by his new lover even though she never tracked his whereabouts or asked for explanations if he was late. However, a woman I know felt rejected unless her lover tried to track her whereabouts. She taunted, teased, and provoked him until he felt sure she was cheating on him, and then he had the phone tapped. Though it may sound odd, that's when she began to feel loved. When such highly charged irrational feelings emerge, rational negotiations are impossible.

Other people can be more rational. One couple, Jennifer and Warren, manage their home life like a business. They are very busy, so they hire a housekeeper, a gardener, and a young woman to take care of their child between three in the afternoon and bedtime. When I met them, they were like two balloons flying high— each with very active careers.

They would coordinate their schedules at the beginning of the week so they knew who would be available to supervise their employees and be with the children. One particularly difficult negotiation occurred when neither could go to their child's piano recital. Unable to change their own schedules, Warren managed to get the time of the performance changed so that Jennifer could, indeed, stop by. There were no accusations, no feeling of guilt, just clear communication and effective action.

You take special care to make sure you have a life of your own, separate from the relationship.

You share some friends, but you also have separate friends—relationships you wouldn't dream of ending, although your partner may not understand what you could possibly see in these people.

A silent pact, made early in your relationship, says, You deal with your family; I'll deal with mine. You both split up on the holidays if your families are expecting you so that neither family is let down. You're polite to your partner's parents, but the thought of calling these strangers Mom and Dad makes you cringe.

Both of you vacation alone at times. Although you might need to discuss it first if your partner wanted to drift off to Club Med for a long weekend, you would probably take off on a ski weekend yourself.

Most of the time you're unaware of a need for greater closeness in your relationship. Maybe you'd give more—but only if your partner gave more, too.

The Positive Side of Exchange Relationships

A contemporary phenomenon, the modern exchange is a two-career, two financial-system partnership. The key feature of the exchange is that both people have a right to their separate identities. Each person cultivates his or her own talents and makes choices that are personally satisfying. That means trying to avoid rigid role definitions, or repeating those of their parents. Men learn how to cook and do laundry and women learn how to handle investments. This vision allows them to develop a capacity to perform in all aspects of their lives. The goal is autonomy.

Exchange couples bring democratic values to love. They want a fair relationship with an accent on personal freedom, and that means the kind of relationship in which no one feels abused or shortchanged. They bring their capacity to negotiate home from the office so managing power becomes an exercise in rationality; the ability to sit down at the negotiating table and come to a fair trade. In that trade, each person protects his or her self-interest.

The exchange is well-suited for people who are frightened of closeness—and many people are in that spot. It's a style that allows for a family life even though it might not be an intimate one.

Joyce and Martin offer an example. She is a pediatrician, he, a surgeon. They are very active in their professional organizations, frequently traveling to conferences nationally and internationally. Both grew up in troubled, abusive families, so they are very cautious when it comes to closeness. Joyce is aware that if she tries to be too close, she "goes numb inside." Martin doesn't think about it very much. There are times when the distance they create makes them feel empty inside, but mostly they get along.

Quite separately, Joyce and Martin keep in touch with their extended families, and they help out when one or another person needs it. They live together but avoid marriage or any kind of financial union. They know enough about their fears to avoid trouble. For now, it works for them.

The exchange has its desirable qualities as well as its trouble spots. To have a relationship in which both people pursue their talents and yet neither one feels enslaved is a remarkable leap for those in couple relationships, given our patriarchal history. Unfortunately, however, if one person wants a long-term commitment, there's a greater likelihood of trouble.

Why Exchange Relationships Break Down

For all its strengths, there's a big risk in an exchange relationship: When it isn't working, separation easily follows. In the words of singer-songwriter Paul Simon, "I like to sleep with the window open and you like the window closed—so good-bye,—good-bye,—good-bye."

Sometimes issues of personal growth bring unmanageable shifts: At forty-two, Clara became interested in exploring her relationship to God. She began taking spirituality workshops and had a series of powerfully transforming experiences.

"It was like a whole new world to me," she said. "But George wasn't even willing to discuss it. I don't know why I expected anything else—after all, he's a scientist. But you would think he would be more open-minded. Anyway, I started meeting other people who had the same passion I do, and in comparison, my life with George seemed empty. I realized that we had never really had much to talk about. Gradually I lost interest in him, and we separated."

But even if two people manage to maintain their relationship, are they getting the best out of love? This type of relationship often becomes disappointing for several reasons.

One of you begins to want more from the relationship.

I have worked with dozens of couples who argue the merits of their exchange relationships eloquently, and I don't doubt that an exchange relationship can work. The trouble is, many of us secretly yearn for a relationship that does much more than work.

In my experience, when a relationship "works"—it's not a battlefield; we each get along and enjoy each other's company—we start wanting more. We start saying things like, I need you to tell me you love me. Why don't we do more things together? I need more excitement. We lead such separate lives.

You might crave more affection. More time together. More intimacy. Your partner's career might pull him or her to the opposite side of the country, and you don't want to follow without a deeper commitment.

Or nature might suddenly present you with a need for a more vital union. Jessica and Dan are a case in point.

Jessica and Dan were so busy, finding a time for us to meet had been a challenge. Eventually, we found an hour in the early morning. Dan flew in from Stockholm the night before, while Jessica was scheduled to speak at a conference the next evening. He had a degree in business administration and was working for a large electronics corporation. She was the designer of a highly respected line of luggage.

Jessica put it simply, "We're thinking about having a baby, or at least I'm thinking about having a baby. Dan's against it. Usually we can find a compromise when we disagree, but how do you compromise about something like this? Time is growing short. At thirty-eight, I'm not even sure I can have a child. I want a family. Dan doesn't. Sometimes I think Dan doesn't understand the meaning of love."

Having a child was a contentious issue because a baby would change the very nature of their relationship. Jessica complained that Dan was only interested in doing his own thing. She hadn't minded before, she admitted. In fact, when they had disagreed in the past—Jessica wanted to ski, Dan wanted to scuba dive—they went their separate ways, marveling at how wonderful their marriage was. But now, Dan was adamant about his feelings.

"You have to understand," he told me, "Jessica is trying to push me into this. I don't have any desire or inclination to raise a child. I'll admit I'm probably too selfish to be a good father."

However, Dan really wanted Jessica to be happy, so during one of their many talks about the problem, he suggested they negotiate and try to come to an understanding. They listed the pros and cons of having a baby. Jessica wanted to feel grounded in family life and have the pleasure of watching a child grow up; Dan anticipated the challenges of being a good father. Then they talked about the disadvantages of having a baby. Interestingly enough, they were in agreement about the inconveniences—more agreement than was comfortable for Jessica.

When Dan pointed this out, he recalled, "She got irrational. She started yelling that all this talk was beside the point. She simply wanted a child. What could I say? So I finally decided it was her choice. 'Look,' I said, 'it's your body. You can do what you want with it. But remember that a baby will change your whole style of life, and don't expect me to be the doting father.'

"She barely spoke to me during the next week. Until this baby business came up, everything was great. Now I'm seeing a side of Jessica I never saw before."

Because these two were in an exchange, neither felt the right to control the other. Jessica had to decide if she really wanted the responsibility of having and rearing a child as if she were all on her own. The choice was hers, and she eventually decided not to do it, which leads to the second reason exchange relationships become disappointing.

You get caught in the lonely-in-love syndrome.

If you are drawn to exchange relationships, chances are you tell your friends, "We're different; none of that traditional nonsense for us." Or, "I'm married, not buried."

What you won't say is sometimes you feel very competitive with your lover. If your partner has a sudden string of successes at work, you worry: Will I become a tagalong to his or her career? When you have a serious career problem, your partner may not be the first one you run to for comfort. You don't want your lover to think of you as a failure—he or she might go off searching for someone else.

In truth, sometimes you feel lonely in this relationship. Consider the argument my client Mark had with his wife the day he ran the Boston Marathon.

"I trained for over eight months for this single event, but after an hour my knee was giving me trouble," Mark recalled. "I wasn't looking to be a hero and spend the rest of the year in agony, but when I got past the halfway point I knew I couldn't quit, even if I had to limp in last."

When he crossed the finish line, Mark's trainer and some buddies from work ran over and tackled him. They stood around laughing, teasing him about his lousy time, until Mark broke away, searching the crowd for his wife.

"I couldn't find Sharon anywhere. Finally I gave up and started home. I walked into the apartment and she was sitting at the dining room table with papers spread around her. I exploded, and she yelled right back at me, 'You know I have a major presentation tomorrow. I saw you start the silly race. What more do you want?'

"The argument we had that afternoon got ugly. I don't expect Sharon to be at my beck and call—and I don't want to be at hers. But if I'm willing to watch her play in her tennis tournaments, she should be willing to watch me run. Fair is fair."

Like Mark, when you work so hard to preserve your independence in a relationship, sometimes you find yourself alone when you need another person most.

When differences are extreme, your goal of fairness and equality fades, and hostility is likely to set in.

Carol, thirty-eight, was dating a man her friends adored, Ron. He had an off-the-wall kind of humor people found hilarious. He was considerate and attractive and very much in love with Carol. In fact, he wanted them to get married.

Ron's proposal brought Carol into therapy. Her concern? Carol was two credits away from her master's degree and toying with the idea of pursuing a doctorate. The last time Ron willingly picked up a book was in college, where he admitted he "wasn't much of a student," although he did manage to get his degree.

This was a side of Ron that drove Carol crazy. She found herself hinting to him that he should take a course in business management and putting him down for making a mistake in grammar. She was hostile at times, realized it, but couldn't seem to stop.

In the modern exchange relationship, whatever we do, we want our partner to be a peer, an equal. It isn't a matter of, if I do this, you'll do that, and together we'll make one whole. It's, I do this, and you'll do this, too. If we pour over the Wall Street Journal and can comfortably discuss the merits of zero coupon bonds versus Ginnie Maes, we're going to be uncomfortable with someone who can't manage his or her checkbook. And if our partner can't compete with us, it's easy to forget about their separate talents and to indulge instead in hostile, demeaning behavior.

Your desire for independence may be covering up a
need for intimacy.

People in exchange relationships are strong and independent people, but most of them have a secret wish: that someone will take care of them; that someone will finally give them the love and affirmation they never had. Many fantasize about finding a person who will rescue them from their overwhelming responsibilities and solve their problems. Their insistence on autonomy and independence conceals what seems like an unacceptable and childlike need to be cared for. So they try to convince themselves that becoming as independent as possible will make everything okay.

But most people need intimacy as well as the freedom to develop their separate selves. When you believe that autonomy is the only way to happiness and love, the intimacy you deprive yourself of will create rumblings of discomfort. Individualism isn't enough. In effect, it puts love off until tomorrow.

In the past you may have often said, "I can't be in a relationship right now; I have to get myself together first." Unfortunately, you never seem to get yourself together enough because constant self-criticism, or "high standards," become a defense—a way to protect yourself from involvements that might lead to intimacy.

Also, if you are drawn to exchange relationships, you might be afraid that you can only be loved for what you can contribute, not because of who you are. Your secret hope is, "If I'm really competent, I'll be lovable." And unconsciously you're afraid that who you are, separate from achievement, isn't enough.

You may never get your deepest needs met.

If you are a woman, you may enter an exchange relationship with a false assumption: If you and your partner allow each other enough personal freedom and autonomy, intimacy will eventually come. But your man might not be interested in intimacy at all.

If you are a man, your false assumption may be that you can find contentment in separateness. You may be avoiding intimacy because you haven't been able to create the kind of safety that allows for it—either in this relationship or in past ones.

An Exchange Relationship Can Lead to a Resonant Vision

The exchange relationship certainly has its limitations, but as we have seen, it also has its benefits. It isn't simply good or bad. It is one answer to the need many people have for a sense of personal freedom and autonomy, even after people fall in love. It offers both partners an opportunity to stretch past traditional gender roles toward a more authentic sense of self.

People in search of resonance draw on certain undeniably attractive features of the exchange, but they do so in a way that mitigates its limitations. For example, the personal freedom that partners can have in the exchange is a powerful draw for the contemporary man and woman. People want it. However, the very words "personal freedom" take on a different meaning in the context of the resonant vision. As you'll see, only with that shift of vision can couples take the leap toward the kind of freedom that allows for loving connections.

There is a way to reach for many of the attractive features of the exchange. That way is through resonance.

How to Tell If Your Exchange Relationship Is Too Distant to Satisfy You

The following statements are clues to the pitfalls of the exchange relationship. Can you see either you or your partner making the following statements?

She: We do well together when we go our separate ways.
He: I can only relax when I'm on vacation without her.

These thoughts suggest the distant nature of the exchange relationship. You may be the kind of person who needs a lot of "alone time." Alternatively, you may fear being so overwhelmed by your partner's needs that you ignore your own need for closeness.

She: If he takes off for Greece with his buddies, I'm going to Club Med.
He: If I'm willing to sit through her business dinners, she shouldn't nag me about going home the second we sit down at one of mine.

These thoughts suggest the fear that someone is getting or perhaps giving more than the other. In an exchange, that worry can permeate a relationship.

She: I feel great bringing home my own paycheck. It makes me feel like an equal partner.
He: I expect the woman in my life to earn her own money. I refuse to be the only one supporting a household.

Partners in a modern exchange expect to be sharing the moneymaking role. They wouldn't have it any other way. Trouble arises when one person loses a job or gets sick.

She: I don't think I could ever have children with him. All the responsibilities would end up on my shoulders, and besides, I have too much going on in my career.

He: I'd like to have children one day, but not right now. Kids are a big responsibility, and I've got more than I can handle already.

Parenthood doesn't easily fit into an exchange union. First, it's hard to add these responsibilities to a relationship that at times seems tenuous. Second, the equality built into the exchange relationship often crumbles under pressure, so you run the risk of following the gender prescriptions that assign the entire child-rearing job to women. Even if you avoid this pitfall, how can each of you do both—rear children and earn money—without feeling overwhelmed?

She: If this relationship ends, I'm going to feel like a fool for hanging in there so long without a commitment from him.
He: I don't see why anything has to change. We're happy. Why make more of a commitment than we have to?

Thoughts like this suggest the tenuous nature of some exchange relationships. Couples don't necessarily become more intimate as time goes on, although they may grow ever more competent at work.

The modern exchange has increased people's awareness of alternative relationship visions. Today, people are more likely to consciously try to create a relationship they think will work for them. Partners in an exchange are not passive in the face of personal problems but active participants trying to find other solutions to their difficulties. And the goal of a more equitable relationship, with a shift away from traditional gender roles, can serve them well. However, people in an exchange are often so focused on their personal well-being that they inhibit the development of intimacy.

Most important, having the exchange vision available as an option, with its focus on personal freedom and conscious living, makes it more likely that partners can also choose resonance.

CHAPTER 3

Merging—When Your Relationship Comes First and You Come Last

> ... We are stripped to the bone and we swim in
> tandem and go up and up the river, the identical
> river called Mine and we enter together. No
> one's alone.
> —Anne Sexton, "Eighteen Days Without You"

When did you first realize you were in love? Chances are, when you couldn't wait to be together. It hurt too much to be apart.

You overlooked your differences: So what if he loves to ski, and I'm afraid of heights? We both love golf. What kept you up talking and laughing until two in the morning was the incredible discovery of all the ways you fit together: "You rented *When Harry Met Sally* ten times? So did I! I can't believe you sleep with the covers over your head; I thought I was the only one who did that. You want a house in the country with horses and sheep? So do I!"

You were no longer alone.

That's what happens to many people during the romantic rush of a new relationship. They're so enthralled by each other that they spend countless hours telling stories and sharing secrets. They stop pursuing any personal direction they may have had and concentrate on being close. It's part of the bonding process.

I decided not to go out to dinner with a friend on a night when I thought he might be able to spend time with me. I wouldn't cut my hair because he liked it long.

I stopped drinking because she didn't drink. It was giving up a lot for a guy who once drank twenty-two cups of beer at a frat party.

She didn't ask me to cancel the trip to Cancun, but I did it anyway. I was going away for a week with the guys to play golf and fish. Usually I can't wait to go, but all of a sudden, I lost interest.

Once their relationships become more secure, these new couples usually widen their circle again to include friendships and activities that used to be part of their separate lives. They may still play in bed until four in the morning. They may create a home life together and have a family. But they also find time for lunch with a friend or for watching football on Monday night.

There are other couples, however, who continue to ignore their special talents and personal interests. They stop playing golf, listening to rap music, or jogging in the park. Old friendships fade. Their relationship becomes a sole priority. Separate friendships and personal development are only possible if they don't threaten the other person or the relationship. Time spent apart is suspect. A drink with a friend of the opposite sex, a late night with colleagues, can trigger tremendous upset.

When a merged relationship is full-blown, partners begin to feel as though they're chained together with links of steel.

But togetherness isn't enough for most people; they also need to lead some part of their lives separate from their partners. Traditional gender roles offer that opportunity for the merged couple. She takes primary care of the children, while he makes money. She develops the emotional side of herself, while he becomes the consummate doer. Partners develop only the side of themselves that's prescribed for their sex. That way there's no competition between partners and little danger of too much contact with the other sex. This is the merged formula for separating safely.

Even today, when most women in merged unions work away from home, couples still follow traditional gender roles. A woman I know makes as much money as her husband, but when their baby gets sick, she's the one waiting at the pediatrician's office while he attends a meeting. They both want her to be the primary caretaker of their child. This means she's putting less energy into her job and delaying her career goals. Unlike her colleague in an exchange relationship, home comes first.

Women in merged relationships who can afford to, stop working altogether. With the man as sole earner, this couple forms the traditional unit that raises children, earns an income, runs a clean, comfortable house, and does community work.

Is Yours a Merged Relationship?

If you can identify with the following descriptions, chances are you have a merged relationship.

Togetherness is a way of life.

Mostly, you function as a pair. Social engagements are with other couples; weekends are spent at home. Your dreams of the future are couple dreams; your vacations are designed for couples. While it's likely you both work, home is the center of your lives. Most probably, it's the style of life that your parents also lived.

One night I had dinner with Henry and Jackie. For me, they demonstrate what togetherness means to the extremely merged couple. Henry adores Jackie, and I can understand why. She's the sweetest woman in the world and takes care of him in many small ways. He's also very committed to her. They use the word "we" a lot.

"We think it doesn't make sense to try to raise children in the city," Jackie said.

Henry chimed in, "We believe that private school is best."

Toward the end of dinner, Henry announced that he had to leave early, and Jackie automatically got ready to leave with him.

"I would feel guilty if I stayed," she explained, even though I had offered to drive her home later.

Henry added, "I can't get to sleep at night if she's not next to me."

Married or not, if you're merged, you're likely to be uncomfortable if your partner socializes without you. An evening with friends or a drink with co-workers, especially if they're of the opposite sex, can be threatening. Why can't you be invited to go along? You don't think that people who are lovers should take separate vacations, either. What's important to you is to be together as much as possible with the person you love.

Your lover is your "other half."

When you say you're in love, you mean you've found a person who complements you—your psychological "other half," the one who makes you feel whole.

This means neither of you tries to be everything. Though you may consider yourself a liberated man or woman, when push comes to shove you feel it's a woman's responsibility to make sure that there's food in the refrigerator, and it's a man's to see that there is enough money to pay the bills. It's a complementary relationship—you fit together much like hand and glove.

At that same dinner with Jackie and Henry, we got to talking about how they managed two jobs and child care.

"In our relationship," Jackie said, "if the baby cries in the middle of the night, I'm the one who gets up and changes him. If Henry does, it's a special favor. His work is so much more demanding than mine, and I can stay home a little later in the morning, if I have to. Besides, we depend on his income to live. What I make is for extras."

Henry also talked about how much better Jackie is at quieting the baby. "I couldn't manage without her."

People who merge are specialized workers. They bring the skills they learn as men or women to the family and spend a lifetime honing them. This means that their personal development is likely to be limited to those specialized skills.

A classic example of how this limits us is in the scene from the movie *Kramer vs. Kramer* in which Dustin Hoffman is walking his young son to school after his wife leaves him, frantically asking, "What grade are you in, anyway?" Maybe that wouldn't happen in your house, but it's a solid bet that one of you would have trouble finding the needles and thread, the insurance policy, or the pictures from your honeymoon, if the other person suddenly disappeared.

The Strengths of the Merged Relationship

The merged vision of today is a direct descendant of the two-parent, one-paycheck, "Father Knows Best" family that was the prevailing relationship pattern during the 1940s and 1950s. The vision seems right to many people because they learned it while sitting on their parents' laps or while watching nostalgic renditions of families on television. Since they know it so well, they can re-create it without much effort. Besides, their parents and grandparents took the same approach, and they, too, believe that what the new couple is doing will bring success.

Their friends are likely to be other long-term, committed, merged couples. This means that when they get together with other wives or husbands, they'll have similar problems. There's lots of support in that. Merged couples are in a predictable, well-respected, well-established type of relationship.

One such couple lives with their two children, two dogs, and two cars in a suburb of Philadelphia. Sara feels certain that her lifestyle is the best one possible.

"I have everything I could possibly want," she said. "And I'm eternally thankful that I'm home when my daughter arrives at three in the afternoon."

If Sara were living in the middle of New York City or San Francisco, she might receive a lot of flack for just those words. Her neighbors might be critical because she doesn't work. But Sara is living in just the right place, so she gets the support she needs.

The split between city and suburb is reflected in the kinds of relationships we form. Those in the city tend to extol the exchange; those outside of the city tend to glorify merging.

Merging meets some other very basic needs. It offers the vision of a committed relationship, a home, children, and membership in an extended family. Unlike in the exchange vision, family togetherness is more important than autonomy. Partners dream of growing old together. They feel themselves connected to others as parents and grandparents, aunts and uncles, siblings and cousins. Thanksgiving and Christmas are the high points of the year because they celebrate just this kind of family life.

When such a relationship works, it feels natural, just the way a marriage is supposed to be. It softens the edge of aloneness that characterizes our human existence. These qualities of the merged relationship are a very powerful draw for many people.

The problem is, the merged vision rarely turns out like that in real life.

Together and Close, But Happy?

If the goal of the merged relationship is a close-knit family life in which all members get the love and support they need, why does it so often end up feeling like a prison?

Penny and Barry are a case in point. What Penny remembers most about her relationship with Barry is how good it used to be.

"We'd be up until three in the morning, and Barry would hold me and say, 'I don't want to go to sleep; I'll miss you too much.' Then he'd cross his eyes and make a face—a thing he used to do to make me laugh when he said something romantic that he thought I'd make a big hearts-and-flowers thing about."

They didn't need movies, or restaurants, or anything else to entertain them. They just needed to be together.

Then along came their daughter, Emily. Penny said, "I hated my boss. There was a freeze on pay raises. So I never went back to work after my maternity leave. Barry wanted me to stay home. He thought it would be better for the baby."

It wasn't having a child that caused two people who once made love in the back of a McDonald's parking lot at noon to wonder whether they'd be divorced by the time their daughter graduated kindergarten. The rift came from the fact that they no longer seemed to want the same things.

"Last weekend I begged him, 'Let's just stay in, the two of us, like we used to.' He said yes, and we spent the weekend reading books, fixing up our house, taking long walks—just being together. I started thinking he enjoyed this as much as I did. Sunday night he looked up from his book and said, 'Do we have any plans for next weekend?'

"I reminded him that we had a wedding to go to Saturday. 'Good,' he told me. 'Why don't you make lots of plans for next weekend so that we're not stuck in again together like this.'

"I barely made it into the bedroom before the tears came—and just kept coming."

When Barry told me his version of their problem, he was almost belligerent.

"Penny's driving me crazy," he said. "I work hard all day, and I need some peace at night, but that's not possible in our house. She's always upset about something. If I stay late at work, I hear about it. If I go out for a drink with my friends, she accuses me of neglecting our daughter. Even when I watch a game on television, she complains."

The night before had been particularly awful. Barry got home late, and by the time they had dinner it was very late. He was watching television for a few moments before going to bed when Penny came into the room and sat down, close to him.

Barry said, "I got up to get a Coke out of the refrigerator, and without being aware of what I was doing, I sat down again in a different seat. Penny started crying, but what stunned me was realizing that I didn't want to be with her. I pretended that I didn't know she wanted to make love, but the truth was I don't think I could have made my body perform even if I decided to try.

"I want to shake her these days. I want to say, What happened to that course you said you were going to take? When was the last time you saw your friends? She has a master's degree, but the only thing she talks about is the kids."

What happened was that Penny had devoted herself so exclusively to the relationship, she looked for so much from Barry, that she was bound to be disappointed in him. No one person can satisfy so many needs. But she had also relinquished the freedom to pursue her own life.

Barry, who seemed to have all the freedom, sweltered in his own prison, trapped by his family's growing dependence on him. He didn't realize how equally dependent he was on his wife's role as nurturer and emotional provider—he just thought if he was belligerent enough she'd stop nagging him.

When Penny and Barry found each other, they found their psychological other halves. However, there were troublesome side-effects: Barry found a woman who wanted him, but in a way that felt engulfing. And Penny found a man who wanted her, but in a way that threatened abandonment.

Couples like Barry and Penny come to therapy with bitter complaints: "I want him to listen to me more." "I want her to stop telling me what to do." "I want to spend more time together." "I want her to stop nagging and let me breathe."

For one to win what they want, the other has to lose big. Although they yearn for a better kind of relationship, they can't conceive of the chemistry of resonance—a union in which they could actually have that room to breathe as well as intimate time together. Bitter and sometimes desperate, they cling even more tightly to their merged vision, often until their relationship breaks down completely.

Why Merged Relationships Break Down

A false assumption underlies the merged relationship: Being close always means being happy. This type of relationship often becomes unfulfilling for the following reasons.

One of you craves more closeness and the other more "space."

Women in merged relationships tend to want more closeness while men want more space.

"I need some time for myself," Stan screamed when Adriane complained that he promised to be home at six but didn't arrive until two in the morning. "Stop bugging me about it!"

"The least you could do is call! I spent the night worrying about you."

Privately, Adriane confided, "I'm so lonely much of the time, I can't stand it. But Stan thinks I'm a nag if I complain. He always asks if I'm premenstrual. I know that's when I feel it the most, but if he talked to me more, it would help."

This particular split between the genders is learned through so many generations that it appears to be natural. If you listen to members of the same sex talking to each other, you're likely to hear a man describe his wife as a "ball and chain" and a woman complain that her husband is dense when it comes to being close.

There are other couples who reverse these positions, so that the woman demands more freedom while the man pleads for more closeness. But they're still polarized. For people who merge, there seems to be no middle ground about this. They get stuck in either/or thinking—unable to visualize being free as well as close.

Partners feel "owned" by each other.

If you are drawn to merged relationships, chances are you tell your friends, "We're so close." What's harder to admit is that sometimes you feel possessed.

The extremely merged union is similar to the codependent relationship that we associate with addiction. Merged partners need each other so much that they avoid the search for a separate self. Each person allows the other to be dependent in a way that interferes with personal development. That's what the vision prescribes.

If we lose our own identity when we fall in love, however, chances are that identity was a little shaky to begin with. Otherwise, we would seek to modify the merged vision so that it offered more opportunities for self-development. Perhaps our parents didn't teach or encourage life skills that foster self-esteem, treating us merely as extensions of themselves. Maybe they abandoned us emotionally or physically. When early development goes awry, we enter adulthood without a feeling of wholeness or completeness. We seek to dissolve the inner emptiness by merging with another person. In these ways, the extremely merged relationship fits some very important personal needs.

But couples in extremely merged relationships often end up resenting each other. Partners may attempt to escape by diving into the television set, traveling for work more than is necessary, staying late at the office, or starting an argument. All of which makes a relationship that's supposed to be long-term and secure start to feel very fragile.

Partners live with the fear of abandonment or the fear of being possessed.

It's not easy living with someone who feels possessed. You can sense the anger in such a person, the potential rejection, even if it isn't expressed. Nor is it easy living with someone who threatens to possess you.

Thelma knew she was holding on to her husband too tightly, but she couldn't stop herself.

"He's like an adolescent," she said. "One night he's out with the guys at a game, the next night he's at the local bar. He always has a reason not to be home, or to avoid his responsibilities. And he always has an excuse. I don't think I ever get the whole story.

"I worry that he's having an affair. Frankly, I couldn't manage that. Being second is not for me. My mother agrees. She's also disgusted with him. She says I should leave him and come home."

As it turned out, Thelma was right. Her husband was having an affair. By the time she found out, she was quite prepared to leave. She didn't give herself, or him, the opportunity to understand why the affair had occurred.

If one person is feeling possessed, it's likely the other is fearing abandonment. The reverse is also true: If one person is fearing abandonment, the other is probably feeling possessed. That's a recipe for trouble.

Traditional gender roles create power struggles.

The merged relationship originally came from another time in our culture—when men were considered the natural leaders of a family. The idea still lingers. So, if you're a woman in a merged relationship, you're likely to think that your husband leads, or perhaps dominates. You might even think that he *should* dominate. If you're a man, you're likely to agree and feel that if your wife gets her way too much there's something wrong. This can become a battle over who is in power. However, according to the merged vision, there shouldn't be a battle; it's certainly not included in any of the "and they lived happily ever after" stories. As a result, people often assume that their anger over these issues is a personal problem—that they're messing up a good relationship. They're wrong. Personal issues may contribute, but the battle over who is in power is inherent in the merged vision.

For example, Kate and Tom were in a merged fight over his parents. Tom contributes to their support, perhaps more than even he thinks he should. But when his mother asks for more money, he can't say no. Kate was furious about it.

"I feel powerless to get him to stop giving so much," she said. "He doesn't even consult me about it. Doesn't he know that his own children need the money?"

To which Tom said, "It's my paycheck. I'll do with it what I want. I have to be in control some of the time. After all, I am the man in the family."

It may look like these two were simply in a battle over how much money to give his parents, but underlying that issue was a conflict over who has the power to make that decision. Old gender prescriptions assign men more power in merged relationships, and women resist—either overtly or covertly.

The battle over power is ongoing.

Ellen tells a familiar story. Exhausted from standing on her feet all day at the preschool where she worked and from typing her daughter's term paper at night, she got to bed just wanting to sleep.

"But David insisted on talking about how our son needs more discipline," she said. "I really didn't want to hear him criticize me for being too lenient, especially when I know that he's too harsh, so I asked him to stop. But he went on and on, like a hammer banging at me again and again. Finally he calmed down, and then he wanted to make love!"

At first Ellen said no. "But he kept kissing my neck, whispering about how excited he was. I finally let him have his way, and after it was all over, I was able to get the sleep I really wanted in the first place."

I asked Ellen why she made love when she wasn't feeling sexual.

"He would have been very angry if I said no. And I thought I did the right thing. After all, that's what a relationship is about— you sometimes have to make sacrifices. I certainly wouldn't want him to look for it somewhere else."

Their sexual conflict and their parenting conflict were part of a larger power problem: Living out the traditional gender roles, merged men and women are each powerful in their separate domains, so David felt he had the right to decide when he and Ellen should be sexual, and Ellen felt she knew the right way to parent their son. When one partner doesn't submit to the other, the battle can get fierce.

In extremely merged relationships, anger can become hostile.

As one partner tries to gain control over the other, he or she may speak or act first and worry about whether it hurts the other person later. Sometimes partners demean each other through sarcasm or ridicule. As one man told me, "I've called her names I can't believe, and I feel ashamed of it afterwards. But in the moment, I'm so angry I can't help it."

Other people explode. If these explosions become common-place, the space between the couple can become riddled with fear. The ensuing shame felt by the one who exploded goes a long way toward diminishing his or her self-esteem. Besides, shouting matches don't solve anything; they make both people feel more alienated.

Others create a tension in the house that can be cut with a knife because they let their anger fester unspoken. A woman may deny her husband sex while he denies her any help with the kids. Each deeply resents the other. This kind of argument can be as devastating as the verbal kind. One isn't better than the other.

Neither partner feels appreciated.

When two people are immersed in their separate gender roles, they begin to have trouble understanding each other. Before too long, her "preoccupation" with the children bores him, and his "obsession" with work is foreign to her. Now the merged romantic dream of "two who become one" is even less likely, and both people feel misunderstood.

Chances are, at least one partner will have a secret fantasy: He or she hopes that something will happen to make the other realize how important he or she is. Perhaps she dreams of meeting someone else and leaving, so that he will feel sorry for the rest of his life; or, he hopes he might narrowly miss having a terrible accident, so that she will realize how precious he is to her. These fantasies reveal a longing for appreciation.

The woman gets caught in the superwoman syndrome.

Because our current economic reality demands that most women work, the woman's traditional gender role may be unreal-

istic at best. At worst, it can create the superwoman syndrome—
and sometimes it's the woman who desires that role!

When Nancy, a forty-two-year-old client of mine, returned to
work, she made it clear that her husband would have to help her
around the house. He did. But she complained bitterly about his
work—he never vacuumed in the corners; he stacked the dishes
wrong in the dishwasher. She would spend more time redoing
what he had done than she would have if she had done it herself.

A control freak? Not necessarily. Unconsciously, Nancy was
very uncomfortable giving away part of her role to her husband.
It seemed to minimize his dependence on her and upset the balance of an extremely merged relationship.

The man gets caught in the macho-husband syndrome.

It's not easy, in this day and age, to maintain the traditional
prerogatives of the male role—the foundations of that role are
fast disappearing. The man may need his wife's money to maintain their standard of living, or she may resist his attempts to lead
the way. Still, some men try to live out the macho-husband syndrome.

At worst, the man might position himself as the only person in
power, even if the context of his life doesn't support it. Trying to
be in control of spending when your wife has an income and a
checkbook of her own is a losing game—that is, unless you use
your power abusively.

Extreme male dominance, in the form of physical or emotional abuse, is a direct result of the merged vision gone awry.
When male power is assumed necessary, which is the case in
merged unions, individuals may use their power abusively. A
man who feels impotent or inadequate to fulfill his traditional
gender role may use every ounce of strength he has to bolster

himself, and that can lead to violence. The results are disastrous for both people.

Everyone's deepest needs go unmet.

Merging can actually interfere with the development of a loving relationship because it leads couples to create unions that are all-important and even engulfing, while their separate selves fade into the background. This has become an important problem in our time, as many women, as well as men, spend a good part of their lives developing their sense of themselves in school and at work. They do not plan to throw it all away once they fall in love. But if they accept the vision of merging as the basis of their new relationship, it actually undermines their unique and separate selves.

Personal development involves furthering our special talents and making choices based on our particular, idiosyncratic interests. However, the merged relationship depends on the divisions of gender roles to create separateness. If we live those roles, we do not become ourselves, but rather we become versions of this stereotype. If we can't live those roles, we're likely to feel like failures.

I'll never forget the moment I learned this for myself. It was 1961. Bob was twenty-six, I was twenty-five, and our first child was six months old. Our son was asleep and Bob was working late when a friend dropped by on her way home from work to say hello.

I remember thinking how great she looked, dressed for work, excited about some new project she'd just been assigned, while I sat huddled under a blanket on our new Scandinavian sofa, tired and tearful.

My friend took one long look at the scene and said candidly, "Barbara, you're depressed—and you have to do something about it."

Preoccupied with the baby, our home, everyday tasks, I had been only vaguely aware that I was unhappy. I thought the problem was inside me. I couldn't really explain my unhappiness in any other way. After all, I thought I had done right to follow the established truths of my generation: I went to college and began a career, and almost as quickly got married, pregnant, quit my job, and had a baby. Never mind that the days were long, that I had little contact with other adults except on the playground, that I missed a work life that made me feel productive and competent. Never mind that most of Bob's time was spent pursuing his career, and he had little energy left for me or his infant son. We were doing what everyone else was doing—fitting into the male and female roles prescribed for us. At the time, these prescriptions were as invisible as the air we breathed, simply part of life. If I was unhappy, I thought the problem had to be me.

The friend who told me I was depressed helped me examine myself and my situation. Fortunately, I began to see that the problem was in the poor fit between me and those traditional roles, rather than a deeply seated psychological disorder. Her comments led Bob and me to take a new look at how we were shaping our lives. It was another important step toward developing a vision of the life we wanted to live together.

Not too long after, I got a part-time job. I have a clear memory of the moment when I handed my entire first check over to the woman who was taking care of our baby. Trading my work for her work didn't bother me at all. I felt very lucky because now I had both things I wanted—time to be a mother and time to pursue my separate life. Bob also decided he wanted to balance work and home in his life. Though it took eight more years, he was finally able to get his first part-time job. We were on the road to resonance.

Changing What Doesn't Work for You

If you see that your relationship has many of the qualities of a merged union, the first step is to see both its benefits as well as its troublesome aspects. Then you'll be better able to evaluate your vision of a good relationship as you move toward resonance. Many of the good qualities of a merged relationship are important for a resonant relationship—one that fosters the closeness you probably expect of your merged union but avoids the loss of your separate self.

How to Tell If Your Relationship Has Become Too Close for Comfort

The following statements are clues to the pitfalls of the merged relationship. Do any of them sound like something you or your partner would say?

She: I know he wants sex tonight; I better find some way of satisfying him or he'll start thinking about finding another woman.
He: If I ever lost her, I don't know how I could go on living.

These thoughts suggest the fear of abandonment, which can cause us to deny our separate needs or the development of a separate self.

She: When he screams at me, I get confused, and I can't even think of what I need to say.
He: If I don't stop her this time, she'll end up trying to control everything in my life.

Thoughts like these suggest that these two are feeling engulfed by each other, and perhaps because of this, there's a battle for power and control going on.

He: She doesn't let me have any time to relax. If I make the money, I should have the right to watch TV when I come home, if that's what I want to do.
She: All I do during the day is work, and when he comes home at night he hardly even speaks to me. Instead, he plops himself down in front of the TV and expects me to wait on him.

Thoughts like these suggest that both people cling to traditional gender roles, but these roles are not working. It would be better if he were able to enjoy the TV and she didn't wait on him. She must also identify her own desires, so that he can satisfy her.

He: I bet if I tell her why I'm worried, she'll laugh at me.
She: Since he refuses to give me more money, I'm going to take it right out of his wallet. I have a right to it!

Open communication is impossible when people don't trust each other. If one person doesn't really expect the other to listen, or to take his or her needs (financial or otherwise) into consideration, it's likely that there will be no open talk. Perhaps they each fear that openness will be used against them later. That's what happens when the battle for control rages in an extremely merged relationship.

He: I want to get away from work when I come home. Besides, she wouldn't understand my problems. She'd end up telling me what to do.
She: He's inside his own head when he comes home, and he's certainly not interested in my work—or the kids.

People become increasingly distant as they confine their separate selves in their separate gender roles. In this way, merging can actually lead to loneliness.

In the next chapter we'll take a look at the resonant vision. This vision offers closeness and personal freedom, a feeling of safety and trust, and a sense of self-respect. Many people long for it. In fact, they somehow expect it even when they're in a merged or an exchange relationship because they don't realize that these two visions have aspects that get in the way.

Resonance doesn't have these troublesome aspects. It's the kind of union that prepares you for the peak experiences of love.

CHAPTER 4

Resonance—When You're Close as Well as Free

... and now you are and i am now and we're
a mystery which will never happen again
—e. e. cummings,
"now all the fingers of this tree (darling) have."

We think we expect too much of relationships. The truth is, most of us expect too little.

We believe that the passion of a new relationship inevitably turns into a dull, depressing, even painful routine. We settle for predictability, comfort, and companionship when we could have the excitement and the sense of well-being that's part of the search for resonance.

You and your partner probably have the capacity to imagine many different kinds of relationships. Together, you can even imagine one in which you each feel free as well as intimate. Just think of the sparks that fly between two electrical wires when they're neither too close nor too far apart, and you can begin to understand what the resonant vision is about.

Resonance is different from merged or exchange relationships because it holds the potential for freedom as well as closeness. By freedom I don't mean the fierce, often isolated, independence that people in an exchange relationship sometimes assume; instead, it's the kind of autonomy that allows each of us to be unique, authentic. And by closeness, I don't mean getting stuck in a prison with a white picket fence. It's the kind of closeness that develops when it's freely chosen.

Autonomy and closeness of this sort are possible when we fully understand that human beings are social animals; for me, this means that the neighbors I live with, the forest that somehow continues to grow above and around me, and the people I love are all part of me, as I am part of them. How I think, the words I use, and what I see and hear are all infused by others. We are one.

Being close is not being afraid of that truth.

The wonder is, we are also free to make a special place for ourselves. We can stretch past the customary and explore our particular "take" on this existence we hold in common.

We can be close, and we can be ourselves.

And each couple can consciously adjust the balance between the two so that the vision fits the needs of both people as they develop.

The more experience I have, the more I understand that couple relationships are a form of art. Once you see your union in a resonant light, and commit yourself to that vision, you will want to make changes in your approach to the canvas. It takes time to get good at it, but guided by that vision, each conscious stroke of the brush brings you closer to a union you will want to live within.

Using the brush consciously means taking a hard look at the merged or exchange messages you have absorbed and avoiding the pitfalls of power and control. It includes stretching toward your full potential and tailor-making a union that fits who you both are rather than who you "should" be. If you also know, as you try to do all this, that nothing human is perfect, you'll be creating a resonant relationship.

In this chapter, we'll focus on understanding the resonant vision. Then in the next chapter, we'll discuss the tools that can be used to make the resonant vision come alive.

What Does the Experience of Resonance Feel Like?

I'll share a personal story with you—about a day at the beach when Bob and I first began to use words to understand the experience of resonance. It was a peak experience for us, one that let us know ourselves when we were at our best. Those few moments, and all the subsequent thought we gave them, clarified our approach to coupling, helped us be more surefooted in our own relationship, and gave us important information about how to help others in counseling.

It began one morning when we decided to take a long walk along the edge of the ocean, even though we needed winter coats to ward off a cold March wind. The beach is a wild place with secrets to disclose, especially before people inundate it during the summer.

The early morning haze blurred the scene so that ocean, sand, and sky melted into each other. The beach was dotted only by sand crabs and sea gulls.

Walking in step, we sensed the rhythmical movements of our hips and felt the recurrent lapping of cool water on our toes. We watched as the waves surged toward the shore and were sucked back into the deep, over and over again, leaving outlines drawn in the sand. Occasionally one of us would speak, and with the slight tightening of an arm around a waist, the other would respond. We instinctively knew that too many words would drown out the ocean's music. At that moment, we were having an experience of oneness, of "we." Stopping a while, I scanned the beach for shells while Bob fed the gulls some breakfast bread we'd saved. We were centered in our separate worlds, feeling free to see through our own pair of eyes.

My attention shifted toward Bob as lots of birds gathered from all directions, darting and diving, trying to catch some bread. He threw a crumb toward one gull an arm's reach away, and we both watched as the bird stretched out his neck to make the catch, retracted his neck to eat, and then looked at us expectantly, ready for more.

I threw the next scrap, and again the bird stretched his neck up for the catch and down to eat. After a while, I realized that we were in a dance together; one of us throwing, one of the birds responding. This was another "we" experience, but now it included the birds.

Laughing with the gulls, we probably looked like a couple of fools to anyone walking by, but at the time I didn't give it a second thought. What was happening was too important. I realized that no one was alone. I was sensing the connection between the rhythm of our bodies and the flow of the ocean, feeling the beat between us, the gulls, and the natural world. To me, that rhythm felt like one colossal heartbeat.

This was the moment when I discovered that we were part of a larger, living whole and that much like the larger whole our smaller union was alive.

A few moments later, we emerged from the experience of oneness, once again separate, once again listening to the music with our separate ears. When we could talk, I was amazed to realize that Bob had made the same discoveries.

I have thought many times about what we felt that day on the beach. The word that came to mind was resonance—an echoing rhythm, a clarity of vision, a sense of oneness coupled with moments of separateness. These were all part of the experience.

I wanted to know why it had happened. Was it the beach, the gulls, the time together?

I've since learned that it was all these things and yet none of them. In fact, resonance is natural phenomenon—every part of our world is both separate and connected—and there's a flow between the two states. It's just that human beings aren't always aware of it.

Very simply put, I've come to understand that when we're separated we tend to take steps toward finding something or someone to feel connected with. That can be another person, a sea gull, or the swell of a wave as it reaches the beach. When we're connected, we eventually have the impulse to step away and know ourselves as separate. This ever-changing fluctuation is built into life. If we can stay in tune with it, resonance is ever-present.

The challenge in intimate relationships is to feel free enough, and safe enough, to be in tune with the reality of resonance. You don't have to fight for either separateness or connectedness. Instead, if you allow yourselves, the two of you will alternate naturally.

Have you ever had a wonderful weekend together and then had an ugly fight on Monday morning? Have you ever pretended to fall asleep after making love because you didn't want to be held or touched for too long?

None of us would have to take such extreme measures if we understood that it's natural to alternate between closeness and separateness. No couple can sustain closeness twenty-four hours a day, every day; one of the partners will do something that breaks the spell. This is a fact of life that romantic movies and love songs would have us forget. Also, no couple can sustain the kind of independence that denies closeness; it starves the union.

It's the fluctuation that's basic to resonance. This is what we learned that day on the beach.

The Roots of Resonance

Though they didn't call it resonance, poets and philosophers have long celebrated a union that enhances both people. Images of it abound in literature and art. These images are as much a part of our lives as merged and exchange images, only we don't often pay attention to their significance for our personal lives.

These images describe a sense of oneness with the larger world, a feeling of stillness that exposes the beauty in and around us, and an awareness of the ever-constant flow between separateness and connection.

These artists and poets know that the peak experiences of resonance cannot be caught in some perfect picture; rather, they come and go. As the poet William Blake says in the poem "Gnomic Verses," "[s]he who kisses the joy as it flies" knows that living well is living in the ever-changing present.

The biblical Song of Songs, here in a translation by Marcia Falk, celebrates this awareness as it sings of the wonder of a sexual union and the eternal movement between yearning. . .

> At night in bed, I want him—
> The one I love is not here.
>
> I'll rise and search the city,
> Through the streets and squares
>
> Until the city watchmen
> Find me wandering there
>
> And I ask them—have you seen him?
> The one I love is not here.

. . . and fulfillment.

> *O women of the city,*
> *Swear by the wild field doe*

Not to wake or rouse us
Til we fulfill our love.

It sings about the experience of oneness that goes beyond being
between male and female.

Like a mare among stallions.
You lure, I am held.

It sings of the beauty of the human body.

Your hair—
as black as goats
winding down the slopes

Your teeth—
a flock of sheep
rising from the stream
in twos, each with its twin

Your lips—
like woven threads
of crimson silk

These are just a few excerpts from one of the most beautiful
collections of love poetry. In it, a male and a female voice both
initiate love. At times, both are urgently craving, aggressively demanding, and tender and soft. They yearn and they are fulfilled.
The poetry ends with yearning, thus accentuating the unending
flow of a loving relationship.

D. H. Lawrence, an author of our century, writes in "Love Was
Once a Little Boy" about other aspects of love—the power and
the intensity of desire, the miracle of being one and being two at
the same time.

The two individuals stay apart, for ever and ever. But the two
streams of desire, like the Blue Nile and the White Nile, from the
mountains one and from the low hot lake the other, meet and at
length mix their strange and alien waters . . .

And he describes the absurdity of the contained, predictable love people call "perfect."

> See then the childish mistake we have made about love. We have insisted that two individualities should "fit." We have insisted the "love" between man and woman must be "perfect." What on earth that means, is a mystery. What would [it] be?—one that never overflowed its banks? or one that always overflowed its banks? or one that has exactly the same overflow every year, to a hair's breadth?
> My dear, it is absurd. Perfect love is an absurdity.

Last, but perhaps most important for me as I try to understand the qualities of resonant relationships, is the contribution of the philosopher Martin Buber. He explores the spirituality that underlies every experience of love. And then he performs the remarkable feat of outlining a path by which we can make that spiritual love a part of our everyday lives.

Certainly, he says, love isn't what he describes as an "I-It" relationship, in which people behave as if the other is an inanimate object without an inner life. Sadly, many people try to love this way—causing themselves and others untold misery and many failed relationships.

Rather, Buber describes love as an "I-Thou" relationship, a connection that is based on a deeply felt mutual respect. Each individual is seen as a spirit-filled subject rather than an impersonal object. God is not only transcendent but inside each of us. Our spiritual challenge is to know this every time we greet each other.

Lovers who relate as an "I" to a "thou," he says, are like a candle lit with a fiery tongue of flame repeatedly separating into two and returning to one. To my mind, this is as close as words can come to describing the experience of resonance.

What Does a Resonant Relationship Look Like?

Most of us have felt something resembling the day-to-day experience of resonance. Maybe you remember a time when you each felt clear and strong and also together. Perhaps it was early in your relationship, when you were first bonding, and you treated each other with wonder and ecstatic appreciation.

What happened in each of these situations is that you and your lover allowed the walls between you to disintegrate—you let go of your defensive and distancing behavior. At the same time, neither of you lost your separate voice; by that I mean, you each paid attention to your thoughts and feelings. Under these conditions, those momentary, peak experiences of oneness are likely to appear.

Marcia, a forty-one-year-old advertising executive with a large, national agency, was married to Steven for more than five years when she had the following experience.

"It was Sunday morning," she said. "The baby was still asleep, and we were cuddling in bed, when Steven said, 'You know, I think lying here in bed with you in our home is the greatest—even better than skiing powder or sunbathing in the Caribbean.'

"I was pretty sure this was a hint that he wanted to back out of a trip to St. Thomas slated for the winter. There was no way I was letting that happen. I really wanted to go.

"So I asked him if he was backing out, and he assured me he wasn't. He said, 'I wouldn't do that to you. But I do think that having a vacation in bed at some other time could be fun.'

"Strange, but the idea stayed with me. What would it be like to have a vacation at home, just the two of us? Did Steven really have a good idea? I knew the choice wasn't just about money. I kind of liked the thought of sending the baby to my mother and unplugging the phone so everyone would think we were away. It felt illicit. And we could use the money saved from the trip for the dining room table I'd wanted for so long.

"A few weeks later, while we were in a bookstore, we found ourselves looking for novels to read during our week at home. We laughed and decided to actually change our plans.

"Keeping our intentions secret, we canceled our reservations and began to dream about languid days beside the fireplace, time for his guitar and my poetry writing, long afternoons for making love, and quiet dinners for two at nearby restaurants. That was five years ago, and I still remember that week. I've never felt so close—and so free to be myself."

How did this happen? It was more than finding time for a week together that made this couple's experience so memorable. To begin with, they managed their conflict well. When Steven suggested a vacation at home, Marcia didn't feel she had to give in or risk his anger. Nor did she put Steven down because he had a different idea. Instead, they took the time to explore their separate needs, and then they played with several solutions.

Steven suggested one: They could put the vacation-in-bed idea off until sometime in the future. Marcia considered another possibility: They could buy a new dining room table with the money they'd save. Slowly, the idea of shifting vacation plans become hers as well as his.

Because they felt safe exploring their individual desires, they were able to imagine a vacation that differed from either of their previous notions but that answered both their needs. They felt the pleasure that comes with the creation of a such a solution; one that enhances each person as well as the union. Theirs was a resonant relationship, ripe for the peak experiences that characterize it.

With greater awareness and insight into the process, most couples can create this kind of relationship and be open to the peak moments that loving at its best has to offer.

Following the Path Toward Resonance

Resonance begins with an important shift in the way you think about your relationship. It includes an awareness of "I" as well as "we" and a willingness to hold both in mind.

Let yourself be close.

A relationship can never be perfect. It will always have flaws. But you need to feel safe enough to expose your personal needs. A safe environment allows you to be close.

Here's a story of how Martha and Ben found their way to closeness and at the same time maintained their safe environment. It began as she was coming home at the end of the day, excited by the conference she had attended. She was excited to tell Ben about it. But she was also yearning to make love.

When she unlocked the door, however, she saw that Ben was asleep on the couch. Lying down, he looked terribly tired and drawn.

"This must have been a stressful day for him," she thought. "I wish I could talk about the conference with him—I like to talk and share things before we make love. But he's not much good at talking when he's like this. I'll tell him about the conference later. Now I need to focus on him."

So she put her briefcase down, sat next to him, and gently rubbed his forehead. He mumbled something about what a hard day it had been and turned over. She massaged his back and told him how much she loved him.

Martha knew Ben was feeling vulnerable and needed to be held. She thought he was wonderful because he would let her do just that. It took a while, but she finally felt Ben's body relax. That's when she whispered that she was free now; they could play in any way they wanted, and the troubles of his day would wash away. Ben didn't respond immediately; instead, he let her words seep through his mind, turning them over and tasting them. Slowly, they made their way to bed.

What happened here? To begin with, Martha desired sex and didn't stop herself from making it happen. She also knew that there are many paths to sex; hers was through words, his through touch, and they could make room for both. There would be other times when the intensity of a conversation would lead them to bed; this time it was her loving touch.

Adjusting but not abandoning her sexual desire, she nurtured their union. Stretching past his preoccupation with work and responding to her desire, he did the same. And no one felt pushed or resentful. There wasn't any hidden anger.

It may look like this happened easily, but in fact it took lots of thought and practice. Martha wasn't so clear about her sexual desires earlier in their relationship, nor was she so adept at expressing them. There was a time in Ben's life when he couldn't respond to her desire without feeling pushed.

As Martha and Ben understood the behaviors that got in the way of their closeness, they could act with greater understanding. This created a safer relationship environment, one that suited their particular needs.

Let yourself be free.

A man once told me that he never felt comfortable holding his lover's hand when they were walking down the street. "This might sound strange," he said, "but holding her hand isn't the problem—it's how to let go." This makes perfect sense once you realize that in order to take the risk of saying yes to closeness you have to be able to say no to closeness.

Martha and Ben tell another story that illustrates their capacity to be free enough to meet their separate needs. They had set a Saturday aside to paint their kitchen, but on the Friday before, Martha said she needed to put it off. Her best friend was in town, and she really wanted to spend the day with her.

At first, Ben was annoyed. He said, "We have an agreement to get this done, and I put the time aside for it. You're blowing me off!"

"Ben, I wouldn't do this if it wasn't important to me. I really love hanging out with my friend, and she's only available on Saturday. Please understand."

After more direct talk, Ben finally did. He sensed how important this friendship was to Martha, and he was able to put his needs and their union on the back burner for a while.

It was a small event, by no means momentous, but it did build trust between them. Martha didn't abandon her own desires, and Ben stretched to meet her needs. He knew that at other times he was the one who needed to be separate. They talked directly about their needs, and no one felt taken. There was no leftover anger or resentment. Each person had the freedom to go his or her separate way—even when they had planned to do otherwise. They were able to say no as well as yes to closeness.

Learn to do the dance.

The key to the flow between "I" and "we" is to think of the resonant relationship as a dance. First imagine that you're on the floor by yourself, feeling the beat of the music deep inside you and moving with it freely and with abandon. As you dance, you get to know your body and how it responds. You learn to consciously express subtle responses to the music.

We learn to be ourselves by continuously exploring who we are, by listening to the music inside of us. What are our special interests, our talents? Are we being true to them? What are the fears that stand in the way? How can we expose those fears, face them, dispel them? Answering these questions might involve tracing the roots of our fears to early childhood. It might involve a spiritual quest.

Then imagine the moment when you become aware that there's someone else on the dance floor with you, someone who loves to dance as much as you do. You take a step closer, and he or she responds in kind. Now you're dancing together, responding to each other's interpretation of the music, enhancing it through your separate understandings. But there's also room in this dance for solo performances, times when you each take the floor by yourself.

We learn to be part of a union by understanding ourselves and our partners. What stands in the way of closeness for each of you? What is frightening? How can you both overcome it?

This dance has no beginning and no end—you simply shift from dancing together to dancing separately for as long as you're alive, knowing that you need to do both and giving each other the freedom to do so.

The shift from "I" to "we" and back again is sometimes difficult, but try to let it happen. When you're having one of those peak experiences of resonance, it happens easily, without any thought at all.

Argue in a way that brings you closer rather than driving you apart.

As a family therapist, I deal with conflict every day. Most of the arguments I hear come about because one person is trying to control the other. That other person usually becomes resentful, and he or she either fights back openly with hostile words and actions or does so covertly through subtle put-downs, emotional distance, or procrastination.

When love is at its best there's no driving need to win an argument. Instead, couples learn to make room for their differences. We tend to be so different—with different families, opinions, interests, and perceptions—conflict is bound to arise. In the resonant relationship, partners learn to work with these differences, creating a sense of safety in the process.

Katherine and Carl are an example. Mother of two, married to Carl for twelve years, Katherine was angry because Carl, a vice president of a public relations firm, was working on Saturdays and bringing work home on weekends. Not only that, in a rush one afternoon he told her he had to travel for a few days, leaving her with the children, the dog, and a job of her own to manage.

Before she could register her feelings, he was running out the door, asking her to water the young plants in the garden while he was away. Sure enough, she forgot, and when Carl came home it was the first thing he saw, and he was angry. By that time, Katherine was clear that she was angry, too.

She said, "I'm angry at being left to manage the whole show by myself—and for so long. It just doesn't work for me."

"It's tough, I know," he said. "But I have to put this time in. And anyway, why can't I be able to depend on you when I'm in a tight place? You could have remembered to water the plants."

"I didn't water the plants," she said, "because I put it out of my mind. I think I couldn't take on one more thing. I'm sorry I didn't say that up front. But I didn't realize what was going on for me."

"I know I'm not here enough," he responded. "I need more free time for myself as well as to be with you and the kids. I really don't want this either."

The talk they had wasn't momentous. There were no earth-shaking revelations, but neither were there any put-downs or threats. Instead, they expressed their feelings directly and began to understand each other. By the time they finished, no momentous decision was made. The truth was that they were both in a tight spot, and there was nothing they could do about it then, even though they knew something had to change. Being open with each other and not putting each other down is a way of handling conflict that, by itself, creates the safety needed for resonance.

Uncomfortable though it is, the very process of dealing with conflict is part of the resonant relationship. Trust is created when you listen to your partner's deeper needs without losing sight of your own, and when you understand how vulnerable you both are and so treat each other gently.

Avoid traditional gender role expectations.

As we saw with merged relationships, traditional gender-role prescriptions often stand in the way of our personal development. Resonant couples learn to look closely at these roles to see if either person is being inhibited by those expectations. It's important for us to discover who we really are and to find a voice that is distinct from the noise around us.

All of this takes awareness and sensitivity. For example, if you were taught as a boy to persist in winning competitions or arguments, it will take considerable awareness for you to learn to share the experience of winning with your wife. If you were taught as a young girl that your father was "the king of the castle," and your role was to keep him happy, it will take the same awareness and sensitivity to maintain your own voice in an argument with a man.

Often these behavioral patterns are accompanied by strong feelings. A man's anxiety about achieving at work can lead to silence and obsessive worry. A woman's doubt about her self-worth can lead to depression.

It's not that resonant couples aren't affected by these gender prescriptions; they can't help but be since gender role expectations are a part of almost every human interaction. But resonant couples create a relationship in which it's possible to change their expectations of themselves and each other. Chapter 8 will provide you with some tools for this effort.

Whenever I think about breaking out of gender prescriptions, I remember Jonathan, a man who enjoyed homemaking. His dream was to have a house in the country with horses, sheep, and several children. Marie fit into this vision very well. Her dream was to have that house and children, as well as a career. And that's just what happened.

I usually think of him in comparison to Sara, who grew up with highly achieving parents. They expected her to be a doctor, but what she really wanted was to be a homemaker and a mother. It took her forty years to accomplish but that's what she finally made happen—with her second husband.

Flow with the phases of the dance.

It's perfectly normal to feel very close to your lover—and then to allow yourself to separate and pursue your own goals. The easier this is for you to do, the more opportunities there will be for resonance.

Resonance is created through mutually enhancing behavior, as two self-respecting individuals pulse from autonomy ("I" experiences) to intimacy ("We" experiences) and back again. Though they can happen in any order, there are different phases to the dance. In the first phase, "We" experiences are absent:

> Jane was at work, sitting at a meeting called to consider a new software package for her department. Allen was on an airplane going south to New Orleans. He was reading some material for a marketing conference he would attend in next few days.

Both people are comfortable being in their separate worlds.

During the second phase, there is a clear but limited sense of the union:

> Jane was practicing her tennis game, thinking about the game she and Allen intended to play together over the weekend. Meanwhile Allen was selecting a tie, thinking about what he liked and what Jane liked.

Each person is living their separate experience. The other is present, if only in their thoughts.

In the third phase, partners have a fully shared experience. As couples, we enjoy having the same responses to a song or a film, or when we care about the same things. It's intense and different from anything we can experience alone; it's certainly different from what we feel with any one else. In this phase, the peak experiences of resonance become possible.

> It was a hot, sunny afternoon in August when Jane and Allen finally got around to digging their garden. They felt their bodies move together, knew the sweat of the work and the feel of the earth together. As they uncovered the brown earth shovelful after shovelful, the promise of green growth and of colorful flowers became ever more real. They laughed as they realized they were hoping to postpone the autumn tilt of the earth.

Make time for the most intense of resonant experiences.

For the peak experiences of resonance to occur, you and your partner need to make time for it. You each need time alone, when you're deeply immersed in a sport you love or some compelling aspect of your own work, so that you can feel the stillness and the immersion that is a personal experience of resonance. Then you both need uninterrupted time together to create a mutually satisfying interactive rhythm, reaching back and forth, from self to union and back again, which is the shared experience of resonance.

This means living some part of your lives away from clocks and calendars. That's not easy given our busy lives. But if you do, you'll come to recognize those moments called "now" time—experiences of resonance uniting our entire world that become clear and immediate.

Simply Searching for Resonance Changes Us

Whether through expanding our comfort with closeness or through developing our inner strength, we change on the path to resonance.

Dreaming together about a relationship that might be possible and holding onto the possibility of this union that you both desire creates an optimism that becomes part of your new life.

Paying attention to your individual development, getting to know yourself as unique and different from your parents or your partner, you'll be open to your separate thoughts and feelings even as you learn to know yourself as part of a couple.

Avoiding the demands of gender prescriptions when they don't fit, understanding that the definition of a "real man" or a "real woman" might actually be a false image of you, you'll begin to live a life that is a more comfortable and accurate self-reflection.

Managing conflict without hostility and using your own anger to understand yourself and your partner better, you'll create a more centered, resonant life.

Whether we are in harmony or at war inside ourselves influences our partners, our family, and ultimately, our world. Realizing this, we can search for resonance, for the still points inside, so that the unions we create reflect that effort. And then, in a circular fashion, these unions themselves will provide a safe and nurturing haven for further development.

In the next chapter we'll take a look at some of the tools you can use to discover resonance. These tools will be important as, in the later chapters, we begin to look at the patterns that tend to block us on the path to resonance.

CHAPTER 5

The Tools of Resonance

I am because we are.
—African proverb

Resonance doesn't often occur all by itself. We need to prepare ourselves and our unions for it. As a therapist and in my own life, I have found three powerful tools that can help us create relationships in which the peak experiences of resonance occur frequently. I've seen many couples who use these techniques develop the safety they need to be close as well as separate. Bob and I use these tools ourselves as a source of creativity and as a means of fostering the change that's essential to keeping our passion alive.

Learning to use these tools takes practice, but I know of nothing more effective for confronting the patterns that block resonance. The tools are *focusing, double vision,* and *resonant intention.* But before we examine these techniques in detail, it's important to understand what is meant by the "patterns that block resonance," since these patterns are what need to be changed.

Family Patterns That Block Resonance

Patterns exist throughout the world, for instance, in the symmetrical shape of our bodies or in the weather or even in the sequence of a string of random numbers.

There are also patterns in our behavior. The most obvious are our daily routines: getting out of bed in the morning, brushing our teeth, putting on our shoes. Even the route we take to work can become so ingrained we are not aware of it as we travel. For further discussions about how patterns occur in nature and through time, see the work of both Gregory Bateson and James Gleick.

Other patterns occur between two people, like the frequency with which they touch, the way they manage conflict, or how they make love. Though these patterns can be complex and less predictable, a couple will begin to follow certain steps: One man kisses his wife automatically when they meet at night, but the only other time they touch is when they move toward sex. Another couple hugs and cuddles all the time, but they can't find another way to touch that is more sexually exciting.

These relationship patterns are like scripts we continually repeat with other people. The most important patterns are rooted in our families and occur when we are young. Often they repeat themselves across generations.

These patterns begin as parents present their children with an extremely important puzzle: How can the children get both the closeness and the freedom (the love) they need to grow up?

Sometimes the answer a child finds works well. Gina, for instance, learned at age five to anticipate when her father would go fishing. As he prepared his tackle the night before, she asked if she could go. Whatever he said, she still would get up early enough the next morning so that she was available. Most times, by six o'clock they were both out on the river. Gina didn't fall into this pattern alone; her father created it with her. And it was a resonant pattern:

She asked, he heard, she followed through, and he responded with love—even when he had to say no. Gina, at age thirty-two, can still ask for her needs to be met and has chosen a man who can respond.

Many other children do not find growing up so easy.

Maureen, thirty-three, remembers when she was about three she fell off a swing in the backyard, skinning her arms and legs. Her eyes filled with tears, and she ran into the house looking for her mother. After what seemed like an interminable time, she found her in the bedroom talking on the phone. Maureen tried to tell her what happened, but her mother didn't listen. When Maureen cried still louder, her mother struck her across the face. Maureen ran upstairs to her bedroom, still crying, but no one ever came to comfort her. When Maureen finally came down, no one said a word about what had happened.

While the actual incident may have been different from what Maureen remembers, what is important is that this incident survives in her memory as an example of what was an abusive pattern between mother and daughter. This was a multigenerational pattern as well: As a child, Maureen's mother's need for closeness was also repeatedly met with physical pain.

To this day, Maureen has followed the same pattern with others, withdrawing whenever she's hurt. The little girl who once went into hiding still does. She's afraid of being hit.

This pattern blocks resonance in two ways: Maureen still tends to choose partners who, like her parents, meet her need for closeness by striking out. Second, the pattern is so powerful that she expects it to repeat even if the other person doesn't become abusive. To find resonance, Maureen needs to find her way out of these responses.

Sam offers another example, only for him the pattern that blocked resonance didn't interfere with closeness but with the freedom he needed to grow up.

> You know, I used to love to play baseball as a kid, and I was pretty good at it, but I was terrible at studying. I have this memory of a

time when I failed a spelling test. My parents sat me down at the kitchen table and told me that I wouldn't ever be able to play baseball again. The thing is, they really meant it. And still, I never did well at school.

The pattern described in this as well as in more minor episodes starts with his father. They used to go to games together and watch baseball on television. Most important, that's where Sam felt he had a natural talent, where he felt the power and the freedom to stretch into a successful young man. When that freedom was abruptly taken away, and his desperate pleas went unheard, he shut down and became sullen.

Now Sam is in his early thirties and he's still shut down. He can't find a job for which he's suited. Somehow, something always goes wrong: He's late too often, he forgets an important instruction, he manages to alienate his boss. He feels very badly about it afterward but that doesn't change his behavior.

It wasn't surprising for me to learn that while Sam's father was a successful businessman, his paternal grandfather was never able to earn a living. Although we'll never know exactly what happened, perhaps he, too, was callously denied the freedom to live in his own way.

As you can see, interactive patterns come down across the generations. Sometimes children act in the same way as do their fathers or mothers, uncles or aunts; sometimes a generation is skipped. An interesting quality of these patterns is that they are the child's best answer to the need for closeness and autonomy. Sam's sullen resistance, his guarded detachment, worked for him when he was living at home—it protected him. He didn't entirely give up his separate voice. His spirit wasn't broken. But that same sullen resistance led to failure once he became an adult. His bosses simply fired him.

The way to undo a pattern is to become aware of it—seeing it not as a personal deficiency but as a family's approach to closeness and freedom. It's a life issue a family has been working to solve for generations.

Just about everyone interacts in a patterned way, even yourself, if you think about it. Some of your interactive patterns get you the closeness or the freedom you need. Others fail. Changing a pattern that blocks resonance involves facing the fears you have around freedom and closeness.

Cultural Patterns That Block Resonance

Cultural patterns also exist. These patterns can be found, altered to fit, in ourselves, in our families, in our mass media, and in our governmental policies. Not only our family patterns block resonance; our larger cultural ones do, too. We are taught, or we observe, many destructive patterns in school, in the media, and even in the acts of our government.

Violence as a solution to conflict, for example, is a pattern that can be found in individuals, in their relationships, and in the absence of laws prohibiting the ownership of guns in this country. Negligent, indifferent behavior to others is a pattern that can be found in parents, in a neighborhood, and in government policies that do not support adequate day care or health care. And resonance is next to impossible without a safe environment.

Another example is the pattern of the image of the hero in our culture. Children watch these stories closely, hearing about athletic stars, or other famous people, who often come from poverty and pull themselves up by their bootstraps. Often, these people are depicted as lone individuals overcoming all obstacles. We're tremendously taken by this image of freedom, forgetting the families, the coaches and teachers, the networks of support that are necessary to nurture such talent. If we think about these people at all, we tend to assume they're standing in the way or taking advantage of the hero.

Our popular heroes often live extravagant lifestyles and marry beautiful people, but their relationships tend to be short-lived.

They are sometimes so committed to achieving for themselves that they know little of the rest of the world, especially about how to love. Besides their remarkable performances, they often give little back to the rest of us.

When our own popular heroes and heroines are emergency-room nurses and firefighters, when we know their outstanding performances are the result of both their present and their past families, and when they demonstrate that the human quest for achievement is embedded in connection, then our images of heroes will be furthering the kind of awareness that makes resonance more likely.

Patterns of Thought That Block Resonance

The very way we think about people can become another barrier to resonance. One such pattern begins when we recognize that people, much like fruits and flowers, are different but then go on to create hierarchies of better and worse human beings.

"My brother's the smart one, and I'm the dumb one."

"My sister was always the pretty one. My mother would sigh when she told me I was plain."

"I can't play with the little boy who lives down the block. He's black."

"You're a woman. You just can't think as well as a man."

"You're a man. That means you don't know how to love."

According to these hierarchies, the smart person is better than someone less smart; the white person better than the black one. When people are branded like this, they often take the negative judgment to heart, believing it to be true. While they may easily hate the others who made the judgment, they also end up hating themselves for being dumb or plain, black or female. This goes a long way toward creating the distrust and the hostility that makes resonance impossible.

Another pattern of thought that blocks resonance is called *either/or thinking:* either you're right or I'm right, either women know the best way to live or men do, either you're free or you're attached. Polarized thinking like this pervades our lives and is the cause of much of the conflict we talk about in this book.

Alex and Vanessa offer an example of either/or thinking. He's an independent soul. He likes to figure things out for himself and doesn't always remember to consult others. On the other hand, Vanessa is always talking to people about her life; forever networking and gleaning information. They're not too different from many men and women in our culture.

"You're impossible," Alex said. "The whole world knows about our problem with a leaky roof. I think this is the third person you called tonight, and it's only eight o'clock! Besides, what would your friend Joyce know about it? I told you, already, I'll look at it in the morning."

"What makes you think you know everything?" Vanessa responded. "My friend Joyce had the exact same problem, and she told me about her neighbor who happens to be a roofer. We might need his help."

Neither person's approach is automatically right or wrong. Alex's approach is to do it himself; Joyce's is to get help. Both approaches can get the job done. However, these two are trapped by either/or thinking, so in their minds, one of them must be right.

Because resonance is a holistic approach to life, we need to use a holistic approach in search of it. *Both/and thinking* means that, if we look carefully enough, both you and I are somewhat right.

Alex and Vanessa could join together so that they had both his skills and her skills available to solve the roof problem. Then he could explore the problem, she could find out about resources in the community, and together they could decide on what to do next. That would mean respecting each person's approach to problem solving.

Whether it be a pattern handed down across the generations of one family, a pattern transmitted by the media, or a way of thinking, if it doesn't lead to a sense of safety and the freedom to change, it's not likely to be the way to search for resonance. And the pattern can be changed.

Three Tools for Achieving Resonance

You might ask, How can I possibly break patterns that pervade our culture or come from my family over many generations? Three tools—focusing, double vision, and resonant intention—can help you face this challenge and so further your search for resonance.

▪ Focusing

The night before Renata moved in with Mitch, she destroyed all her old love letters. She said, "It wasn't fear that he'd stumble over them in a drawer someday and have a fit. It was my own feeling that I was with Mitch now and I should forget everything in the past."

Many of us think we should give up certain parts of ourselves to be with someone else. Sometimes we not only try to bury the past when we come to a new relationship, we almost try to recreate ourselves completely every time we fall in love. We forget that our relationship patterns follow us. We're anxious to be what someone else would have us be, thinking that's the way to be loved. It's little wonder that we often lose touch with ourselves.

This also happens when we are afraid to look inside ourselves, shamed in advance by the flaws and the fears we suspect are there. However, the peak moments of resonance occur when no one part of ourselves is suppressed, when we aren't trying to avoid thoughts or feelings.

One woman sat before me struggling mightily to hold back her tears. She didn't want to show me how sad she was, but more important, she didn't want to show herself. This internal battle, the disquiet and the shame, takes up so much psychic room there's little left for sensing the joy in life.

Focusing is a tool you can use for getting in touch with your inner self. It can help you know who you are, so that when you relate to your partner, it's with a clear sense of your own thoughts and feelings and with an awareness of the patterns that shape your life. We'll make use of a process suggested by psychotherapist Eugene Gendlin in his groundbreaking book *Focusing*, which conceptualizes your "felt sense."

You might find it easier to understand how to focus if you imagined you had a magnifying glass built into your mind—once you catch a thought or a feeling, you can get up close and learn more about it. The focusing tool can help you observe thoughts as they pass though your mind and understand feelings as they emerge in your body. This will help you discover the patterns that shape your relationships.

Step one: Listen to your "inner voice."

Focus inside yourself and become aware of your inner thoughts. You'll hear your internal commentary on everyday life—the ideas that cross your mind, your musings on a quiet afternoon. By focusing on them, you can separate enough from the flow of everyday life to observe your mind in action.

At times your thoughts may sound like the child or the adolescent you once were. Other times they will sound just like what one of your parents would say. Often they will reflect the competent adult you are now.

You have all these different kinds of thoughts because ever since you learned how to talk, and even before, you began to register what was happening around you. Experiences don't simply disappear, they're stored in memory, and when correctly triggered, they reappear. If you listen closely, you can develop an observing self—and learn much from this.

Judy, an extremely overweight woman with a congenital heart problem, began to listen to her inner voice in an effort to learn how to eat well. Soon she realized that there was a battle going on inside her even when she thought about food.

Certainly, she could hear the part of herself that was self-critical say, "You eat like a pig. I can't stand looking at you. You're fat." These words sounded remarkably like those her father used to shout.

Judy could also hear another part of her respond belligerently, "I deserve some treats after all the work I've done during the day. I've been good. Besides, no one, no one at all, is ever going to stop me."

The battle that once raged between her and her parents was still going on inside her. As she focused inside, she heard her parents' panicky shouts, and she also heard the tremendous power in her response. Judy carried this family pattern inside herself. But it was leading her to an early death.

Often what we think about ourselves and what a parent thought of us becomes a muddle. Focusing inside, Judy discovered this confusion. In the process of differentiating, what she thought about herself and what her father thought about her became distinct and she developed a more separate self. She took responsibility for her eating pattern, and so it became easier to learn how to eat well.

To practice listening to your own inner voice, choose a time when the outside world is quiet—early morning or late night are often good for this. Then listen closely, particularly if what you hear has anything to do with a current concern or problem. Don't worry if your attention wanders; when you realize you've drifted off, just refocus.

Listen to your thoughts and describe their tone. Does the tone remind you of someone else? Of yourself in the past? Of one of your parents? In this way, you can explore your own mind. Perhaps it will help you recognize a troublesome pattern.

Step two: Access your "felt sense."

In addition to your inner voice, you can also get to know your "felt sense." You may not be aware of it, but if you're hungry or thirsty, anxious or joyous, your body feels it. Many people have trouble accessing their felt sense because, in our culture, we tend to rely on what we see rather than what we feel. But you can learn to be aware of it.

For example, Philip loved speeding around sharp curves, especially when it was late at night and he wasn't as afraid of being caught by the police. It was only after he smashed into another car, and he and several people ended up in the hospital, that he really understood that this pleasure was also a serious problem.

Lying in the hospital bed, he now had the motivation to access the feelings that emerged in his body when he drove. He discovered that his chest expanded and his heart beat faster whenever he imagined himself speeding. He felt exhilarated—it was pure joy. But almost immediately afterward, he heard his inner voice say, "You're just an irresponsible kid. Grow up." And then he felt his body grow heavy, as if it were a burden just to be alive.

After getting in touch with these bodily sensations and the thoughts that accompanied them, he could recall having had them many times in the past. His mother and his father often used those very words, and his wife used them after the accident. And he could certainly recall the bodily feelings. It was a pattern.

Though there was an easy solution for Philip—he could just blame his family for making him feel bad—that wouldn't change anything. Instead, he had to realize that all those body sensations were his—part of a pattern he had inherited—and only he could change them by learning how to manage his craving for speed.

Take the time to pay attention to your felt sense. Some people can tune into it directly; others can do it after focusing on their inner voice.

Learn what your body has to say when you have a troubling or a happy thought about your relationship, or when something important happens that affects your union. Perhaps your shoulders will feel tight or your head will hurt. Maybe a sense of peaceful relaxation will sweep through you. Gather all the information your felt sense offers. It is an honest, very personal, authentic expression.

Mark is a man who used the focusing technique as he dealt with his part in a relationship problem. He is married to Betsy, a woman who is brilliant in her law practice but was completely nonathletic, the type of person who literally falls over her own feet. Mark, who swam, golfed, and worked out at the health club three times a week, tried everything he knew to get her involved. Betsy wasn't interested. They followed a pattern that kept them apart.

Then Betsy's law firm did some work for a company that sponsored a team of cyclists for the Tour de France. As a bonus, she traveled to France to meet the team. She was fascinated by the young athletes and their dedication, and she bought a bicycle on her first weekend home.

Betsy began to ride with a woman's group on weekends. It became a passion—one her husband, who had weak knees, couldn't share at all. A year later she was riding in fifty-mile events, some of which took her away for weekends. That's when the trouble at home started.

"It's an addiction," Mark told her, pulling out an article on exercise addiction he'd clipped from a magazine.

"It helps me get rid of tension, and I'm losing weight," she explained.

"You're never home anymore," he argued.

"I thought you'd be proud of me," she countered.

They both realized they'd reached an impasse. The pattern that kept them apart had intensified.

"Focus inside," I suggested to Mark during a therapy session. "When she goes off riding, listen to your inner voice. See if you can access your felt sense."

Mark listened to his inner voice and found it was consistently critical of his wife: "She's not coordinated enough to be an athlete. She's neglecting the house. She's neglecting me. Maybe she's getting ready to find another man."

As he looked for the felt sense behind these words he realized that there was an alarming uneasiness that spread through his body. It was almost as if he wanted to jump out of his skin.

Soon Mark was able to understand that while he had resented his wife's lack of interest in athletics, he had also been comforted by her disinterest. Betsy's new passion had triggered his fear of rejection.

When his wife left for another cycling trip, Mark was more aware of the uneasiness in his body. He couldn't sit still. She had this new passion; all of these new friends. He was bored with the health club; bored with his life. She was changing. He was the same. Would they still connect?

With a greater awareness of his feelings, Mark could now do more than complain. He could find a passion of his own, confront his sense of stagnation, and take steps to add more stimulation to his life. He could explore his fear of rejection, dipping back into the past to understand its roots. He could also share with his wife his internal discoveries, and they could try to find another balance between their separate lives and the life of their union. Hopefully, he would do it all.

Use the focusing tool to get in touch with what you think and feel, and then bring what you learn to the union. That will help you create a resonant relationship.

▪ *Double Vision*

Double vision is a process that is at the heart of resonance. Double vision allows you to break out of your own patterns so that you can grasp the thoughts and feelings that your partner brings to the relationship. It's the capacity to keep your own truths—perceptions, needs, dreams—in mind while taking in your partner's separate truths. At its best, double vision allows you to move toward a both/and pattern of thinking.

To practice double vision, you must consciously put your own truth or opinion on the back burner for a short while. Many people have trouble doing this even for a moment, as if setting aside their opinion will make it disappear. They fear they will lose themselves in the process. Alyson and David are two such people.

Late one afternoon, they began to argue. It was Friday night, and she had plans to go out to dinner with friends. He had wanted to go to the movies together.

"You didn't tell me you were going out to dinner," he said with some disappointment in his voice. "You know I look forward to being with you, especially on weekend nights."

Alyson responded from her own feelings, saying, "I can't stand it when you expect me to give up my friends for you. You know it's important to me to be free to do things with other people. How can you forget it, especially after all I've told you about how my first husband tried to own me?"

"Why can't you ever do something I want once in a while?"

It went on and on until Alyson screamed, "Stop it. Stop it. I can't listen anymore. I refuse to give up my night with my friends."

So the argument ended, for the moment. But Alyson was tense and frustrated, and David felt misunderstood and lonely.

Later, I had Alyson and David replay their argument practicing double vision. I asked them to take turns expressing their own needs and then temporarily to set them aside. Then they would be ready to listen fully and openly to what their partner was thinking and feeling.

Being open to your partner's opinion doesn't mean you will, or should, automatically agree, or that you will start doubting yourself. Your own truth doesn't disappear. It's just on the back burner.

When David got angry at Alyson for making Friday night plans, she first responded by affirming her own truth: "You know it's important for me to be free to see my friends. I've said that before."

David repeated her words so that she knew he understood her. This second step is called mirroring. He said, "I understand that you feel it's important to feel free to see your friends."

Once Alyson was clear that at least the words he used were accurate, David talked about his feelings. He said, "I really want to be with you at night, especially on weekends. I feel lonely when we aren't together on a Friday night." Alyson then mirrored David's statement.

Then David took the third step, which is asking what I call the double vision question. He said, "Tell me more about why it's so important for you to make weekend plans without me." The question is designed to increase your information about the other person's motivation.

Alyson talked about her first husband, and what a jealous man he was. Making separate plans was important to her to maintain a separate life. She also felt that as a woman she needed to affirm her freedom at times. She wanted to explore what that meant.

David heard her out without interruption and without arguing. He realized that when she made other plans on Friday night it wasn't, as he originally thought, a rejection of him.

Alyson also asked the double vision question of David, and he answered, "I was always alone on weekends. My parents were busy, social people, and I was their only child—a kind of afterthought. It's a sore point for me."

As they talked in this way, Alyson realized he didn't want to own her. They corrected their errors in perception and made room for each other's truths. Neither tried to dissuade the other or dismiss the other's feelings. They both ended that part of the conversation feeling understood.

Now they were ready for the fourth step in double vision—the search for a solution that would answer his needs, her needs, and the needs of their union. They needed to engage in both/and thinking.

The double vision solution is not possible if you use the either/or pattern of thinking: "I'm right, you're wrong, and I can prove it." This is the kind of thinking that leads to increased frustration and loneliness.

If you find yourself thinking that there's only one "right" solution, see if you can imagine the possibility of many solutions. In the search for the kind of union that supports resonance, neither person's needs can outweigh the other's. The task is to look for ways to affirm both approaches. That comes through both/and thinking: "We're both important here. Let's look for a solution that makes both you and I right."

Then brainstorm solutions using both/and thinking. Sometimes brainstorming results in a solution that is simply a compromise; it doesn't feel great, but simply good enough. At other times brainstorming transforms the problem entirely—the solution becomes a new synthesis, like a chemical reaction that results in a new compound—and it does feel great.

Ultimately, Alyson and David brainstormed several solutions. Every other Friday night could be set aside for separate friendships; they could let each other know beforehand about weekend evening plans with friends or colleagues; they could also pay attention to their Saturday night together, making it a special "date."

By the time they were finished, however, they felt so good about themselves that they had added still another solution, this one for the coming Friday night that had caused the argument. After Alyson went out for dinner with her friends, and David played pool with his, they planned a late-night drink together. This felt right to both of them because it resonated with the relationship vision they both shared, a vision that included time for personal friendships as well as time together.

To practice double vision with your partner, try the following: Recall a conflict you've recently had. Listening to your inner voice, clarify your own thoughts and feelings. Are you angry? Frightened? Insecure? Hurt? What is your body telling you?

Now, put these truths aside for a moment. Ask your partner what he or she thinks or feels. Don't assume you know. Listen to your partner. Give him or her time without jumping in or arguing. Listen and try to understand rather than judging. Both of you should take time to do this.

Then each of you brainstorm by making a list of as many solutions as you can imagine. Don't be satisfied with the first idea you have. Try to list several, even some that seem absurd. Make sure they satisfy your own needs and what you hear are your partner's needs. Ask your partner to do the same, and share what you've learned.

■ *Resonant Intention*

The couples I know who live in a relationship that fosters resonance do it purposefully, with intention. It doesn't simply happen by accident. Resonant intention commits both partners to discovering old patterns, changing them, and doing the kind of dreaming and envisioning that can lead them both toward being the best they can be together. Resonant intention depends on the cultivation of one's will, and both Roberto Assagioli's *Psychosynthesis* and Rollo May's *Love and Will* describe this well.

Resonance relies on a vision—part healthy fantasy, part reality—of a relationship that allows for freedom and closeness. Your resonant intention supplies the energy to do the job.

Dream together.

Sometimes we make light of our imagination, believing it's a waste of time. Nothing could be more wrong. Hope is trusting that your dreams will be fulfilled, that if you're open to opportunities, they will arise, and you will welcome them. With positive thinking like this, wishes become the building blocks of the future, the stuff out of which we create our lives.

For instance, two people who are in a new relationship might share the dream of being able to travel together for a whole year. For them, the imagery itself is bonding. They might plan where they would go, the adventures they might have, and the risks they could take. Hoping for the opportunity, they are more likely to make it happen, or at least some rendition of it. Wishes and dreams are a kind of nourishment, a food. And those who don't dream go hungry.

So use your resonant intention to dream up a future together. Envision the kind of house you would like, the amount of money you want to earn, the way you want to relate to each other. You can envision yourselves in the country or in the city, with children or without them. What dream, risk, or hope guides you toward the future? Use your focusing tool, test out how good these wishes feel. Ask your partner to do the same exercise. Use your double vision to understand each other. Brainstorm a way of making room for both images. Remember, the more resonant your intention, the more resonant your future.

Play together.

I can't overestimate the importance of purposeless, "as-if" behavior, when we act as if our dreams are real. The playful child "inside us" is a source of many feelings, much creativity, and at times, pure joy. The world of make-believe enriches our lives.

I will always remember the couple who played together by acting as if they didn't know each other when they met after work at a bar. They kept the fantasy alive all evening, ending up at a local motel for the night, without their children.

Creating opportunities for fun, and setting aside time for breaks from everyday life, gives you the opportunity to enact impulses that adults ordinarily put aside. Free from obligation, alive in the moment, it's more likely to be a time of resonant connection.

You can "play" in many enjoyable ways: Dress up and go out, acting as if you had no other responsibility in the world. Go to the mall and pretend you both have a million dollars, and show each other what you'd buy. Take a bubble bath together. Go dancing; see a ball game. It isn't what you do that's important, but that you have no other purpose for doing it but enjoyment.

Plan for your needs.

Map out a way to save money to buy a house. Consider a way to deal with Christmas so that your family can celebrate it meaningfully. Restructure your life so that there is time for each other. These are all examples of conscious, purposeful thinking. As long as nobody feels forced, it will work.

For instance, one couple spends every Tuesday night together no matter what, because they feel their relationship needs its own special time. This is their strategy for making sure they get it.

Return to your wishes for the future of your relationship. If you and your partner have envisioned them together, share the task of creating a strategy for achieving one of those wishes. If you've done it by yourself, create the strategy yourself. Consider the money needed, break down the necessary tasks into steps, decide who will do them.

Most important, don't fall into the despair trap. If it feels like too big a wish to manage, take on a small part of it. Alternatively, try a different, more manageable wish.

Putting It All Together

We are creatures of pattern. Some patterns lead toward resonance, others don't. Focusing inside brings awareness of old patterns, of who you are and what you want; double vision, or the capacity to empathize while maintaining your own sense of self, brings closeness; and resonant intention helps you to use those new awarenesses to shape the future. Used together, these skills move you toward resonance.

In the chapters that follow, we will look at the different patterns that shape relationships. Becoming aware of the ones that foster a resonant relationship, you can stretch toward them by using the three tools introduced in this chapter.

CHAPTER 6

Power and Control

Who is the slayer, who is the victim, speak.
—Sophocles, *Antigone*

Who has the power in your relationship?

Think for a moment. Whose "no" is always listened to, whose ignored?

Who decides if you'll go out tonight? Which mutual fund to invest in? The model of the new car? The children's colleges?

Who apologizes first? Who signals that the discussion is at an end? Who gives the second chances?

Your answers may shift from day to day, or from one situation to the next. On the other hand, who holds the power may be painfully clear, like in the case of the man who told me, "It's her way or the highway."

No one likes to think that they're trying to control the people they love, or for that matter, that they're being controlled, but the struggle over power plays a part in most relationships. In fact, trying to gain control of others, and nature, is the primary way we use power throughout our culture.

The attempt by one person to control another person is most blatant in merged unions. In the extreme, people rank each other according to personal characteristics—by gender, wealth, intelligence, or talent—and those who are considered "superior" try to dominate those considered "inferior." The word "power" is derived from the Latin *posse,* meaning "to be able," and the Sanskrit *pati,* meaning "Lord" or "possessor." So power has been related to the rule of the male for a long time. This idea causes no end of trouble in close relationships.

The exchange relationship is a remarkable leap forward for couples when it comes to power. Partners consider themselves equal. At their best, they negotiate mutually beneficial agreements. It's a more democratic form of family life. No longer does one person rule; instead, partners rely on a set of agreements. When they're in conflict, they try to negotiate a fair trade. The trouble is, the fair trade is a very rational approach to power, and human beings can't always sustain it.

I know a couple who agreed to split the chores around the house so that neither person takes advantage of the other. If he does the laundry, she cleans the kitchen. It's a fair trade, and it works. Unfortunately, when the going gets rough between them, and their anger swells, they often lapse into the attempt at control.

Resonant power is radically different. It is based on mutual trust and the desire to empower each other. Resonant power uses both/and thinking and disregards any judgmental hierarchies related to gender or wealth or earning power. Under these conditions, power becomes collaborative, a product of two.

How does a couple get to the point where the shift to resonant power is possible? How do they ready themselves so that it's less an ideal and more a reality?

The first step is to realize that power in one form or another plays a part in every single relationship. No use denying it, there's not even anything resembling a conversation without some distribution of power.

The second step is to dispel the myth that one person needs to be in control for a family to work smoothly. Domination may be more efficient, but in close relationships it leads to resentment, anger, and open rebellion.

The third step is to become aware of how the attempt to control gets played out in your relationship.

Who's in Control?

Elizabeth Janeway, in her book *Powers of the Weak,* outlines two ways that we try to control others—overt and covert.

Overt control is more obvious:

• You've given him the ultimatum: He either marries you, or you'll never see him again.

• You say, "I refuse to go anywhere with you dressed like that!" when you dislike her outfit.

• You are your partner's calendar—you remind him of the people he needs to call, the shirts he has to pick up, the dental appointment he needs to make.

• He's slicing onions for the spaghetti sauce, and you grab the knife out of his hands: "I said minced, not chopped!"

• You're helping her control her spending by confiscating her credit cards and hacking them into little pieces.

Covert control isn't immediately obvious. Often it's wielded without any self-awareness of the desire for control. Anger and even resentment can be so well hidden, they're almost absent. However, this kind of control can be just as powerful as overt control. Consider these examples:

• You're hurt that he didn't ask you out last Saturday night. All week long you dodge his phone calls; you let him sweat and wonder where you are until he's calling five times a day.

• She sounded cold on the phone and you know she's mad about something. You show up with a dozen roses and quickly change the subject when she brings up the problem.

• You take his mother to lunch and complain about his temper, expecting that she will be on your side in the next fight.

• She reminds you that you promised to help her unpack the boxes in the basement tonight, but you miss the last decent train home.

• You have a secret money stash your husband doesn't know about—just like your mother did.

• He raises his voice an octave, and you race from the room in tears, making him feel guilty for yelling at you.

Men are often trained to become experts at overt control, but certainly there are also women who learn this role. However, even though we often become brainwashed into believing that overt power is absolute, this type of power is the product of a collaboration between the partner in power and the others who participate. The one in power often forgets this and, at least on the surface, so does the so-called "powerless" one.

I always think of the partner in overt control as another rendition of the emperor without any clothes. He or she struts and shouts and perhaps abuses others. But even slaves eventually rebel. And when that happens, the emperor's vulnerability is exposed. Power in family life is always a product of a collaboration, usually unconscious.

A couple I know were in a battle over money. He demanded that she account for every cent, while she managed to "siphon" considerable money into a private account. He sat her down for long budgetary lectures; he looked in her wallet to see what was left. Then he ranted and raved. But she continued to savor every dollar she saved and the secret power it gave her. While his behavior was overtly powerful (he apportioned the money, planned for and monitored its use), she continued to undermine him. The truth is, he couldn't be in absolute control. It's impossible. But because he didn't know that, he assumed the problem was a reflection of his personal "weakness." His wife's covert control made him feel impotent.

While men are usually trained to use overt control, women often become experts in covert control. This type of control also has a price to pay. To begin with, people often don't realize that covert control is a form of power; a person who uses it unconsciously might still think of him or herself as powerless. Also, because covert power is based on deception (which most of us consider unfair or unsporting), it's also destructive of self-esteem. Indeed, it's not playing by the accepted rules, but of course, those rules have been established by those with overt control! So if you use covert control, you're likely to think poorly of yourself, even if it works.

A woman I know used her covert control in a match with her tyrannical boss. He demanded his way and even raged at her for not following his orders. But more often than not she managed to get what she wanted because she was an excellent strategist. When he wanted more room for a new associate in the office and asked her to move her desk to a less central place, she declined, arguing that she would be less accessible to him. When he demanded that she fill out the same time sheet everyone else used to account for their work, she conveniently forgot. Those who felt threatened by her success called her "ambitious" or "manipulative." Although she liked getting her way, she felt diminished by the way she did it—especially when she heard how others described her. When I asked her if she had power in her office, she looked uncomfortable and said she didn't feel as though she did.

The One-Up/One-Down Argument

Think about how overt and covert control play out in your relationship, but realize that this power dynamic has been all too well learned by most of us. It's pervasive in our culture. The person who is one-up has the weapons of overt control, and the person who is one-down has the weapons of covert control. The benefit is that they both know the taste of power. It seems to offer both safety and freedom.

Gayle and David are an example of how this culturewide pattern works. For the past five years, Gayle has made the arrangements for their ski trips, with little help from David. Making the plans, she feels in control, powerful, one-up. Once they arrive at the mountain, however, David undermines her. He asks, Why did you choose this hotel? It's too far from the lifts. Why did you get a rental car? We could have taken the shuttle. Did you know we have to go all the way into town for breakfast? Well, don't you think you should have asked? After this, David feels powerful and one-up, while Gayle feels frustrated, criticized, and one-down.

They have repeated this same pattern on many ski trips. Why? Gayle is a woman who needs to feel in control to know that she is free. Unconsciously, she seeks people and situations that will allow her to fulfill this need. David is her perfect match—at least until they arrive at the mountain—because he needs others to take control. Unconsciously, he avoids responsibility so he won't make any mistakes. At first, this keeps him passive and one-down, but after they arrive he recoups his losses by second-guessing Gayle. Without being aware of it, Gayle and David connect through this pattern.

Consider the one-up/one-down pattern of Janice and Ron. They usually see each other several times a week, but then suddenly, for no apparent reason, Ron stopped calling. After three days, Janice was seething.

Ron finally phoned when she was dressing to go out with her friends on Friday night. "Listen," he said, "the meeting broke up early, so I'm coming over."

Holding the phone in one hand while putting on makeup with the other, she thought, "How dare he assume I'll drop everything at the last second, just because he's suddenly free! Does he think I sit around my apartment, staring at the walls and waiting for him to call?" She told him she already had plans.

He said, "So change them. I'm leaving town in a couple of days. Can't you see your friends then?"

Janice held the phone away from her ear, waited until his voice stopped, and then hung up with a loud click.

"The funny thing is," she said later, "I really wanted to see him. But when I think a man is trying control me, I get so angry I feel the hairs rise on my neck."

Five days passed, and Janice didn't hear from Ron. She left a message. Another week passed. By then Janice was frantic.

"I don't know what gets into me sometimes. If only I could reach him, I know I can make him understand."

This episode began when Ron stopped calling for several days, and Janice felt one-down and rejected. When he did call and she hung up, she became one-up and so felt safer. But the pendulum swung back rather quickly when he once again pulled away, and she was left feeling rejected once again.

Dana and Scott are a final example. One year, Dana's entire department was out celebrating the end of the company's fiscal year. At five minutes after twelve, she glanced at her watch and thought of giving Scott a call so he wouldn't worry. But then she figured he'd probably been asleep for hours. A little voice in the back of her mind also said, "It won't hurt him to realize that he can't control me all the time." She felt threatened by her husband's need to possess her and wanted to find some freedom.

When Dana arrived home, Scott was wide awake. Without any conscious attempt to threaten him, she admitted that George, a man she worked with, drove her home. Scott exploded. "You're a whore. I know you want to sleep with him. Admit it!" He threatened to hit her.

Now Dana felt frightened and out of control. She tried valiantly to convince him she hadn't done anything wrong, but he yelled and threatened her until she fell to the couch, sobbing. Then he left the house. At four in the morning, he returned drunk and burst into the bedroom demanding sex. Not too long afterward, he passed out.

When he awakened the next morning, Scott rubbed his head and tried to fight off the guilty suspicion that he went too far the night before. Dana looked calm and detached.

"You're a wife abuser," she told him. "I really think you were close to hitting me last night. I never imagined myself married to a man like that. I should leave you; I really should. If I stay, who knows what will happen next!"

In this situation, Dana began in the one-up position by contending that she was free to stay out late and associate with other men, and she became one-down when Scott threatened to hit her. However, when Scott woke up with a headache and the guilty suspicion that he went too far, Dana was again in the one-up position.

The safety Scott thought he could have by being one-up didn't materialize—he couldn't control Dana without the risk of losing her. The freedom Dana thought she could have by being one-up backfired—she couldn't control Scott without the risk of triggering abuse.

Being one-up, and having overt power, comes with a storehouse of very powerful weapons, enough to tyrannize and mistreat. That's a dangerous predicament for the person who is one-down. It can even lead to defeat and an end to the one-up/one-down battle.

In all these examples, however, there is an ever-shifting contest between one-up and one-down. These couples are in merged relationships, and so one person assumes the right to control the other person's behavior. The other often resists, particularly when their safety or their self-esteem is threatened.

The Control Fantasy

Why do we try to control the people we love? First of all, deep inside, most of us have a fear of being unsafe—that comes along with being human. Being in control gives us the feeling, false though it is, of being safe in an unsafe world. We spend considerable time and energy trying to protect ourselves. But the attempt to find that safety through the control of another person ultimately fails. Most people find ways to rebel.

Second, control helps assuage fears of abandonment and engulfment. When we want to feel needed we might think, "If I give her free rein with her money and she manages it well, why will she need me?" When we want to feel free we might say, "If I don't take control and make the vacation plans, I'm not free to do it my way." These are very common human fears that can only be quelled temporarily through control.

Third, we tend to confuse our power over things with power over people. For example, if I hit a tennis ball with some measure of skill, I can control the direction it goes and the speed at which it leaves my racket. The tennis ball isn't going to talk back or change direction in midair because it decided to go elsewhere. But we don't have the same powers of control over human beings. If we try to control those we love, they ultimately find ways of talking back. Whether overtly or covertly, they chart their own course.

Do You Need to Be in Control?

Perhaps you're aware of your attempts to control your partner, either overtly or covertly. Most of us fall into this trap from time to time, and often we're unclear about how to get out of it. "If I don't do it, it won't get done," one man told me as the reason he bosses his wife and children.

If you're in this trap, ask yourself these questions: What makes you need to be in control? What anxiety does it soothe? Where did you learn it? What is the payoff? What is the price?

There are several possible answers to these questions:

You and your partner learned the one-up/one-down pattern early in life, and you know no other way to deal with power. As you repeat the pattern, you're continually warding off your partner's overt or covert control. Even if you're one-up, you pay the price by being subtly undercut. You frequently have the thought, "Where is he or she going to get me next?" I know plenty of couples where the so-called stronger person begins to feel completely helpless as the other person gets better and better at undermining him or her.

You don't really trust your partner's love or commitment to you, perhaps on an unconscious level. Your attempts at control are your way of protecting yourself so that he or she can't hurt you. The hidden benefit of always being the one in control is that it's reassuring not to have to lower your defenses. The price you pay if you don't risk trusting another person is that you will never put those fears behind you.

One price you pay for trying to be in control is that you're likely to feel lonely. Somewhere inside, something will feel like it's missing. When you are always trying to be in control, there's no chance to share your deepest feelings, no opportunity to be vulnerable and scared. You're always so busy guarding yourself that you've forgotten what trust and safety offer.

Perhaps the biggest price you pay for the kind of power we call control is that it's destructive of your union. The union you and your lover create is alive, a whole that's bigger than the two of you. When either of you diminish the very self of the person you're trying to love, you also diminish the union. In the long run, you also diminish yourself.

Resonant Power

The antidote is learning to use resonant power, which means rejecting the one-up/one-down pattern and substituting the both/ and pattern. To do this, you must nurture your inner power and become aware of the tremendous influence you have on your partner. Awareness of this influence will make you less likely to feel threatened by your partner's strength and influence. The result? Decisions are the result of two and feel right to both of you. This goes a long way toward developing your resonant union.

Power is found both inside you and between you and the person you care about. The power that is inside you is a natural result of life experience and of learning to value your own thoughts and feelings. You become centered in who you are and can express what you want or need. Developing it is a lifelong process. That's inner power.

The power that is between you and the person you care about is naturally part of your relationship. You necessarily influence and are influenced by your partner. Being open to that influence is a tremendous leap forward in the development of a union—it's the foundation of resonant power.

The miracle is that resonant power already exists between you. You have power and so does your partner, if you can recognize it.

To understand what I mean, imagine for a moment that you and I are in a close relationship. Being close means that I care about you. Once that happens, it matters what you think of me, and that means you have the power to influence my life. And once you care about me, it matters what I think of you. I now have the power to influence you.

Once we care about each other, we both have power. This is a truth we fully understand when we're in resonance. We feel empowered and we empower each other.

If you and your partner have managed to minimize the destructive effects of control power, you probably have experienced resonant power. Even if you're in a relatively troubled relationship, you might remember a moment when you felt stronger because of the other person's love or solved a problem because of the other person's understanding and insight.

Resonant power depends on your shared capacity to be open to each other's influence, to handle that influence without undercutting it or giving in just to please. Resonant power also depends on your capacity to use your own influence robustly but without disempowering your partner.

You may have lost your sense of inner power. Perhaps you wonder if you ever had it. You may have never acted with the knowledge that both you and your partner have power in your relationship. But you can take steps toward both these kinds of power by using the techniques of focusing, double vision, and both/and thinking.

Use focusing to feel empowered.

We all need to nurture our inner power. The best time to do this is when there's a decision to be made. Find a quiet place and draw an imaginary boundary that separates you from others. This process is for you alone. Then listen to your inner voice. Learn to observe the thoughts that rumble around in your mind. Try to distinguish other people's thoughts from your own. You'll know which thoughts are authentic as you access your felt sense—when you have an idea that "feels" right, it's yours.

For example, Julie came to me for counseling because she was having difficulty making a decision about whether to take a promotion. She always worried what others thought, so making any kind of decision didn't come easy.

"I feel like I have to take the new assignment because my boss won't understand if I refuse. She believes that a woman has to take whatever opportunity comes her way. And I know Randy will never understand. He wants me to take the job because it will bring in more money."

Julie was always taught that others came first and that paying attention to herself was selfish. After years of thinking this way, her own thoughts and feelings, her own needs, were mostly unknown to her.

I recommended that she begin by drawing a boundary around herself and the job decision. For the next week, she agreed not to ask others for their opinions about the new job.

With the boundary in place, she began to recognize which opinions were hers and which belonged to others.

She learned to use her felt sense to test for authenticity. "Close your eyes," I said one day, "and imagine taking the promotion. See yourself saying yes to your supervisor. What do you feel? Scan your body for reactions."

"My whole body grows heavy when I think about this job," she told me. "I don't feel excited. I feel tired, sluggish. That's the real truth."

After a few more minutes she concluded, "It makes me realize how hard I've been working for the past four years. I don't feel like taking on another big challenge. Besides, I've had to put so much of myself on hold. The other day I walked by this little shop in town, and there was a sign in the window offering courses in weaving. I'd like to do something like that. I love working with my hands. Funny, but when I hear myself saying that I won't take the promotion, I actually feel good inside. That's also the truth."

In this way Julie strengthened her inner power. Setting her boundaries, keeping others out, accessing her own feelings, she discovered what she really wanted and began to feel empowered.

Use double vision to access resonant power.

Resonant power is a function of "I" as well as "we." It's power that comes from inside you and power that comes from your union. Julie got better at finding her inner power, but she was deeply involved with Randy. What do you do when you feel your inner power, are clear about a personal direction, but you're in a relationship with another person who might not agree?

Julie could have chosen to act independently. She could have turned the job down without talking to Randy about it. But that wouldn't have worked in their relationship. For the next six months Randy might have waved bills at her, nagging and frightening her until she believed she'd made a mistake.

On the other hand, Julie could have buried her feelings and taken the job to please Randy. Most likely, and I've seen it happen many times, he would have had to listen to her complain every evening and would have ended up wishing she'd never taken the position to begin with.

Instead, she and Randy used their double vision to work it out. Double vision can help you find more than one way to understand a conflict. Julie took the first step, which was to express her feelings.

She said, "Randy, I'm feeling angry at you because I think that what you care about most is the money, not what the job will mean to me personally."

Julie's second step was to listen closely to his response, and not interrupt.

At first Randy responded defensively, "How can you say that? I think you'll like the job. It's new, it's different, and it's a step up. You keep complaining about how bored you are at work."

But eventually, since he'd practiced double vision, he got around to mirroring what she had said: "I know you think I'm too concerned about the money and not enough concerned about you."

Julie was then able to ask the double vision question: "Is that true? Tell me what else you feel."

"I don't think you're paying attention to our finances," he said, "and I worry about that, but I do care about you. I want you to be happy at work. That comes first."

Julie mirrored Randy's concern, so he knew she was listening: "I hear that you worry about the money."

Now it was his turn to ask the double vision question. He asked, "Do you really care about what I feel? Or do you only care about being happy at your work?"

Julie explained that she wanted to go at a slower pace for a while and how important that was to her. But she was also concerned about the money. She wanted to know more about the state of their checkbook. As they looked at it, Randy pointed out that for the last two months they had spent more than they earned. If they continued in that pattern, they were in for trouble. Julie began to appreciate his worry.

What he said influenced her, as what she said influenced him. Neither put the other down. They listened closely. They held the other's needs and perceptions in mind as well as their own. They managed this part of their conflict well.

Now that they had used their double vision to understand each other, the last step was to find a new solution—a new way of thinking that would empower both of them.

Brainstorm to find both/and solutions.

Feeling your inner power and with the understanding that comes from double vision, you're ready to brainstorm a both/and solution. At best, this synthesis won't be simply a compromise that leaves each of you feeling partially deprived, but it will feel better than anything you came up with before. You'll know if this new synthesis is right because you'll both feel content.

I like to think of brainstorming as music: You hear your partner's idea and express your own, finding a way to combine both to create a richer, fuller composition. On and on the process goes, and with every new sound, a new harmony emerges, one that speaks to each person's needs and, finally, sounds right.

Julie began and said, "How about budgeting for two years instead of one? We're both expecting raises, and your salary will jump by 15 percent after you finish your degree."

Randy turned that idea over in his mind, and finally agreed that it was possible. They did have savings to fall back on, if the future didn't turn out as they expected. But he wasn't fully convinced. "I don't want to go through our whole savings. How about playing it safe by renting out a room on the third floor?"

Julie hesitated for a moment. She didn't like the idea of another person in the house, but she tentatively agreed so as to help solve the cash flow problem. Still, it felt like a make-do compromise. Then she hit on another solution.

"I wonder what would happen," she said, "if I took on that new job slowly, one part at a time. I wouldn't feel pressured that way. I'd feel even better if I had two weeks vacation before I started—then I can do that weaving course I told you about. I wonder if it's possible."

She thought for a moment before continuing. "I'm going to talk to my supervisor. They really need someone with my skills. I bet she'll let me do it my way."

Julie and Randy bounced ideas back and forth until they came up with a new way to approach Julie's promotion—a both/and solution. At first they planned to reduce their spending, rent a room, and use savings. Julie wouldn't have to take the new job, and Randy wouldn't have to worry about money. But in the very process of working toward this solution, Julie discovered another approach to her promotion that felt better, and it became their new synthesis—the result of their brainstorming.

When you feel personally empowered, it's more likely you can empower your partner. Then you can build on each other's creativity until you find the both/and solution that feels good to you both. That's resonant power in action.

Working Through the Trouble Spots

When I first introduce the concept of resonant power to couples, I often encounter feelings of disbelief, as if such collaboration is impossible. The whole idea may seem strange because it goes against many of our cultural beliefs, such as that someone must always be in charge or that we must make our own decisions regardless of our partner's feelings.

Resonant power is different, and even revolutionary, for many relationships. It's natural to be a little skeptical, but I can guarantee you that nothing will give you a richer experience or better allow each of you to be your personal best.

Here are some of the most common objections I hear, along with some tips to get you through the trouble spots.

"It's too hard to talk to my partner. If I say what I feel, it will come out too angry, and we'll get in a worse fight."

Anger is a part of every relationship. Expressing it can actually help you understand yourself and your partner better.

Go slow.

Start by focusing inside yourself. Anytime you feel angry, stop and listen. See what your body tells you. You might keep a journal to keep track of what the feeling is about.

One woman did this, and she learned that her anger was mostly directed against herself: "I'm amazed at what a hard time I give myself. I'm always putting myself down. That's my major problem."

Read the next chapter on anger. Talk about what you learn with a friend. Talk about it with your partner. Try some of the exercises in the last chapter. You might find better ways to deal with yourself and ways to approach others with your anger.

"I'm afraid to ask my partner for what I need."

Perhaps another way to say this is that you're stuck in the one-down position, and your partner remains one-up. Unfortunately, that leads to trouble, so it is important to face your fear. Again, go slow.

Fear is a powerful bodily reaction. You probably know it in yourself. Try to catch the feeling when it happens. Focus on it and see what thoughts pass through your mind. Write them down. Often when you look at them later, they don't seem so overwhelming. See if the feelings become less powerful over time. Test yourself by asking your partner for something you need. Talk about your effort with him or her. If, after this effort, the fear is still great, seek help.

"If I pressure my partner, he or she will probably leave me. "

If you expect that your partner will leave you, you are probably using your power, either overtly or covertly, to hold on very tightly. This might make your partner feel possessed, triggering a desperate need for freedom. Then your fear of losing him or her might become a reality.

Did the fear of abandonment develop in your childhood? Do you have any memories of feeling rejected or left behind? Talk about it with a friend. Many people have such experiences. And when you're ready, try talking to your partner about what you have learned. You both might reach a better understanding. Try some of the exercises in this book with your partner. See if you feel safer.

"Talking, brainstorming, listening—sounds great, but it won't help me get my way."

You may have become so good at using your power to get your way that you don't see the price you're paying. Unfortunately, "getting your way" leads to your partner trying to do the same, and that leads to war.

Next time you have a decision to make, see if you and your partner can learn how to use double vision. The goal is to stand clear and centered in your perceptions and at the same time be open to your partner's thoughts. The way to do that includes patient listening and mirroring each other's words. Then you might try looking for a solution that works for both of you.

"I'm not happy with my relationship, but I've tried to make it better before, and it hasn't worked. Besides, this sounds like a lot of work."

Relationships take conscious effort. If you don't really believe that things can change, or if you've tried a hundred times and failed, finding the energy for this effort can be difficult.

However, human interactions can always change. If you haven't succeeded in the past, you can always try again. Perhaps this time will be different.

A woman came into counseling as a last resort. She was ready to give up: "He'll never change. Why should I bother." Only after she realized that her despair was getting in the way was she able to put in the kind of effort that really made a change.

Staying in a relationship that doesn't satisfy is not a good alternative. Risk the hope that it can get better. Try to see if the two of you have the courage to dream again. Read the book together. And seek the help of a professional counselor, if you feel you need it.

CHAPTER 7

Anger Yes, Hostility No

> It is easy to fly into a passion—anybody can do
> that—but to be angry with the right person to the
> right extent and at the right time and with the
> right object and in the right way—that is not
> easy.
>
> —Aristotle, *Nicomachean Ethics*

Karla and Mark were standing on the curb, waiting for the cabdriver to unload their luggage, when Karla's hand flew to her
mouth in horror. The airline tickets were at home, in the top
dresser drawer, where they'd been since the travel agent had sent
them weeks ago.

"When I told Mark I'd forgotten to pack the tickets," she said,
"I thought he was going to hit me. 'You stupid idiot. I don't know
how anyone could be so dumb,' he shouted. He was swearing,
calling me names. By this time the skycaps were staring, and even
the cabdriver, who was waiting for us to pay him, looked embarrassed.

"The airline gave us new tickets—they were really nice about
it—but from Chicago to Denver he cursed me out. He told me

how he couldn't believe he married someone so stupid, how I never did anything right, how my boring conversation embarrassed him in front of his business associates."

Another couple, named Jim and Heidi, told a similar story. Jim said if he had known the discussion about whether to go out or stay in on New Year's Eve would cause such a rift, he never would have brought it up. But, as it was, after two minutes, he and Heidi were in a shouting match.

"I begged her," he said. "'Can't we discuss this? Can't you shut up for two seconds and let me talk?'

"'So talk,' she said, but the second I started to explain, she continued attacking me. When she's mad she doesn't care what she says, or how much it hurts.

"I started screaming, 'You don't want to talk. You just want to score points.' I got my coat and walked into the hall, praying the elevator would come quick.

"She followed me out, swearing and yelling. I could almost feel the neighbors, hiding behind their doors, listening to us. I was terrified that someone was going to call the management office again. Last time she got so loud someone called the police."

Conflict is the hard side of close relationships. Because we see things differently, misunderstandings will always occur. We can't avoid them—nor can we avoid the anger that comes with them. Anger is a natural expression, a source of information, and when handled well, an opportunity for greater closeness.

If I were to summarize in a single sentence the most important principle I have learned as a family therapist about anger, it would be this: You can't avoid your anger, but you must avoid hostility. Anger can lead to peak moments of understanding, intimacy, even transformation, but when it turns into hostility—as it did for Heidi and Jim over New Year's Eve and for Karla and Mark over a pair of forgotten tickets—the possibility of resonance is destroyed.

How Well Do You Handle Your Anger?

He's more than an hour late, and now you'll have to sit in the first three rows of the theater, something you hate because it gives you a blinding headache. When he comes through the door, what do you say?

You get to work and a colleague asks you, "Didn't you get my message?" But you didn't. In fact, you had no idea she had called, and she never would have bothered you at home if it wasn't an emergency. What are you going to say to your partner, who took the message and forgot to tell you about it?

Of course, you'd be angry in either of these situations, and you'd have a perfect right to your feelings. But would you become destructive and hostile? Would your partner?

It's important to recognize the difference between anger and hostility. Anger is a welling up of feeling under conditions of threat, a reaction for which you are personally responsible even though it was triggered by something or someone else. Hostility, on the other hand, is the demeaning behavior that people use when they try to defeat another person.

Anger is, "I'm frustrated (irritated, furious) that you forgot to pick Kerry up from school—I had to leave work in the middle of a meeting!"

Hostility is, "You are the most irresponsible, childish man I ever met and one hell of a lousy father." Hostility demeans not only the other person, but the union.

Think of your union as something alive—like a pond rippling with wildlife or a city overflowing with people. If poison seeps into the pond, not only will the fish die, but so will the whole environment. If a few people in the city kill and riot, the entire web of connections that holds the city together is infected.

Relationships are also living organisms. When partners treat each other badly enough, they destroy the web of connections that holds them together. If they tear away enough strands, they stop caring, and their union dies.

I've seen couples living in dead unions; they live in a barren landscape, destitute and empty, with nothing of value to save. I've also seen couples who treat each other well; they live in a world of good feelings and loving actions. When a union thrives, so do the people living within it.

Unfortunately, when people are angry, they often lash out either physically or with words. In our culture, with our Wild West emphasis on guns and vengeance, we give ourselves permission to hurt the very people we love. Sometimes we do it blatantly and at other times so subtly neither person realizes the hostility behind the words.

We easily enter into what James Joyce in *Finnegan's Wake* calls "the continually more and less intermisunderstanding minds of anti-collaborators."

Hidden and Not-So-Hidden Hostility

It's important to know what to avoid when we become angry. The following forms of conflict are hostile.

▪ Name Calling—Throwing Stones

"You're a stubborn bitch!"

"You're a nasty pig!"

Whatever caused this fight, by the end, both people are seriously wounded—and feeling very unsafe.

Hurling words like these, people can denigrate almost anything about another person, including his or her gender, race, ethnic heritage, or intelligence. Name calling isn't simply letting off steam; it's a powerful, destructive weapon.

▪ Threatening Abandonment—The Harmful Good-bye

A man once told me he never considered himself hostile because he never, ever raised his voice. But quietly and softly, he frequently threatened to leave his wife. While lying in bed together, he repeatedly talked about how dissatisfied he was. While taking a walk or driving to the mall, he described all the younger women who were attracted to him. For many years his wife blamed herself, but ultimately she was the one who demanded that he leave.

Often a partner threatens to leave as a way to gain control over the other. The threat may have little to do with any clear intention to actually leave. The threat can be physical ("I'm packing my bags and calling a lawyer") or emotional ("I don't know why I stay around when you act like this").

Threatening abandonment is one of the most lethal of the hostile weapons because it can trigger raw fears left over from childhood. Because all of us were once infants in need of constant care—and our parents, no matter how good, couldn't always anticipate our needs—somewhere inside we fear being left vulnerable and alone in a dangerous world. Taking advantage of that fear, even without meaning to, is hostile.

▪ Threatening Engulfment—The Harmful Squeeze

I know a woman whose nightmare is that she will be left by her husband. When she was a child, her mother left when she was four. So to keep this from happening again, she tries to possess her husband's entire life. She's jealous of his male friendships and watches his eyes every time a beautiful woman walks by. When they're angry at each other, she frequently demands that he stay awake during two- or three-hour-long harangues in the middle of the night.

Trying to own someone never leads to the safety either person needs. Instead, it generates anger and resentment and the real possibility of abandonment.

Threatening engulfment ("If you don't stop spending, I'll take your credit cards away") triggers some very basic fears. As children we only slowly gained control over our own lives, and to try to control someone again is hostile.

■ Put-downs and Sarcastic Remarks—The Joker

Ridicule, in whatever form, communicates contempt or disgust, and that's powerfully undermining. Such remarks are sometimes delivered in the form of a tease or a joke, so it's hard to detect the hostility: "Oh come on, I was just kidding; don't be so sensitive." Or sometimes the put-down is stated so matter of factly that the hostility is easy to miss. But listening closely, it's possible to sense when the tone of voice doesn't fit with the hostile nature of the words.

A woman I know often teased her husband about the size of his penis when they were in the middle of sex, especially if she didn't have an orgasm. He retorted by teasing her about her weight. By the time they came in for counseling, they had given up being sexual together. Night after night, each huddled on his or her side of the bed feeling lonely and rejected.

■ Disconfirming Another's Reality—The New Historians

Some people regularly rewrite history. According to them, whatever you saw and got angry about didn't happen. Perhaps you're angry because he had ten drinks and slid down under the table in the middle of dinner? If this man were a new historian, he would comment, "What in the world are you talking about? I only had three. It's your imagination."

Therapists call this "disconfirming another's reality." It's about all those times when one person, believing there's only one way to see the world—their own—turns to another and says, "You must be insane or something; how can you think that way? That's not the way it is."

A woman I worked with once saw a damp spot on the living room ceiling, so she climbed up a ladder and confirmed that it was a water leak. Then she asked her husband to help her trace its origin. Because he felt inadequate to deal with the problem, he put it off. When he finally got around to looking, he, too, climbed the ladder and touched the spot, but he did it quickly, felt nothing, and concluded that his wife was simply imagining things.

Another man did a similar thing. He came into the kitchen after his wife had cleaned and made himself lunch. In the process, he spread the same dishes and the same papers that she had just organized. When she complained, he tried to avoid her wrath by claiming she had never cleaned in the first place. However, by denying her reality, he sent her into a rage.

▪ Triangulation—Us Against You

Triangulation is a term therapists use to describe what people do when they make use of others—parents, children, friends, neighbors, the clerk at the convenience store—to win an argument. Having got a confirming opinion, he or she proclaims, "They all agree with me!"

One couple was having trouble being sexual, so they avoided each other by getting into fights just before they got into bed. Often those fights included reports of comments from Clarissa, their ten-year-old daughter. The woman would say, "Even Clarissa told me she thinks you're weird. She doesn't want you to come to parent-teacher night. She said you embarrass her."

Clarissa was used in this way, and the next day she would have to face her angry father. But the argument had nothing to do with her. Triangulation is a form of bullying. The validity of the other person's perception is denied and blame is shifted to a third party.

Why Lovers Become Hostile

Why do some people need to win an argument so badly that they will be destructive to the person they love?

We think it's healthy to "let it all hang out."

"Let it all hang out" is an old saying, left over from the sixties. It originally meant the full expression of our feelings, beliefs, and identities. And it is true that expressing our feelings is one key to good physical and emotional health.

But I've also heard people say that venting all our thoughts and feelings—even if they're hostile—is an essential part of an "honest" relationship.

My common sense tells me that's wrong. Let's imagine a man has spent the evening dredging up his wife's shortcomings. I don't think there are many women who would be able to end the evening feeling, "Oh, sure, he called me a fat pig, but now that he's gotten his feelings out about my weight, I feel so much closer that I can't wait to make love."

Holding a few choice observations back until you calm down isn't deceit, dishonor, or a cop out. It allows the time necessary to consider how to express your feelings in a way that keeps them yours, and so doesn't demean your partner.

We have learned that winning is the only way to be strong and losing is weak.

A man taught as a boy to "win" a fight with his playmates may have a difficult time sharing the experience of winning with his lover. A woman taught to be "right" as a child may have trouble knowing that her lover may also be right when they're arguing. Underlying cultural values teach us that there has to be a winner and a loser.

When we feel like we're losing, we take out our big guns so that we can win at all costs. Rather than shifting to both/and thinking so that both people can be somewhat right, we move toward hostility. We make a last-ditch effort, thinking that putting the other down will make him or her a less powerful opponent in the future. But this will also mean that he or she will be less effective as a person, and a less loving partner. We can win the battle and lose the war.

We're frightened of losing someone we love, or of losing ourselves.

Somewhere inside, no matter how competent or accomplished we are, we all know the fear of losing someone we love. And we also know the fear of being possessed by someone else—and of losing ourselves in the process.

When a lover triggers either of these basic fears, we tend to close down and become more guarded. Then we have less, not more, capacity to respond creatively. Instead, we become simple folk looking for simple answers.

Avoidance fuels this process. Closing down, many people never learn how to manage the anxiety and confusion that fear produces or even come to understand what it is they are afraid of. They don't allow themselves to focus on the fear itself, perhaps because they were never taught to listen to their inner voice or access their felt sense. So they run away before ever really understanding the internal associations that prompted the fear in the first place. They don't develop the self-knowledge and the self-love necessary to manage anger without hostility.

Then it's all too easy to respond with blame—thinking that it was the other person's intention to cause us fear or hurt, when that may not have been true. All of this makes winning seem like a matter of survival—and then the weapons of hostile warfare become easier to use.

When Someone Intends to Hurt

What if the argument isn't something that either of you can be reasonable about? What if your partner is so angry that he or she does intend to hurt you?

Sometimes people can't stop being hostile. Too panicked to look at what they fear, they escalate their behavior until it's beyond their conscious control. If that happens repeatedly, it's important to seek the help of a counselor.

However, most people can work on managing conflict so that it isn't destructive. Even if they start out being hostile, they can learn to avoid it and go on to develop the courage to face their fears. It's an important step in the search for resonance.

Larry and Amelia planned to go away for the weekend. Larry was supposed to return home after work to pick up a suitcase Amelia had packed the night before, and then they would meet downtown at her office. They left late the next day. About twenty-five miles west of the city, Amelia asked him to stop the car so she could get to her suitcase and find her sunglasses. That was the moment when Larry realized he'd forgotten to go back home to get the suitcase.

He quickly apologized for his mistake. "I know I forgot, and I'm sorry. We'll have to go back and get it."

But Amelia was furious. She said, "This isn't the only time something like this has happened. Remember when you forgot to pick me up at the train station, and it was one o'clock in the morning? I've never been able to rely on you. You're so irresponsible. You're like a little kid."

The truth is, Amelia scared Larry when she attacked with such fury, so much so that he had the impulse to stop the car and walk away. Because he had been working on this response to anger in therapy, he could take a moment to focus inside. He feared Amelia didn't love him, that he was simply a convenience to be used when necessary.

He managed to ask a double vision question: "I feel like you don't love me, that you only care about the things I can do for you. Please tell me that isn't so."

Amelia answered, "How can I love you when you're an irresponsible airhead? You should be able to follow some simple instructions, but you can't. As far as I'm concerned, all you're good for is a paycheck."

The worst happened: Amelia confirmed his fear that she didn't love him. At this point he could have easily counterattacked. The words were on the tip of his tongue, but he took a deep breath, and instead said, "Let's take some time out. I don't think I can talk about it right now without getting hostile myself."

To her credit, Amelia was also able to take time out. The anger between them simmered silently as they drove back to the city, but there was no more hostile talk. Later, after they picked up the suitcase and were well into the country, she began again, this time without hostility.

"When I found out you forgot my suitcase, I realized how frightened I get when I'm reminded that I can't always rely on you."

Larry talked about resenting some of her demands. "When you ask me to pick up your dry cleaning, to stop and feed your cat, to make your appointments, I feel like you're using me to do the things you don't want to do."

Before they reached their destination, they could understand each other a little better. They also knew they had a serious problem, and there was a good chance that this kind of hostile conflict would happen again. However, they avoided hostility once, and that gave them the hope that they could do it again.

Managing Conflict with Resonance

You can't avoid conflict in your relationship no matter how deep your love is. But suppose you could use this conflict to reach an understanding deeper than you've ever had? Suppose conflict can lead toward a union that fosters the best you both can be? Suppose it leads to creativity, self-esteem, and a more exciting relationship? This is the promise of resonance.

Managing conflict with resonance is a skill that can be learned. It demands that we take the risk of being true to ourselves—and true to the union.

To get a better idea of how this works, picture the following.

Brian and Cara attend parent conference night, and it's a nightmare. "Terry can do the work," the seventh-grade teachers assure them. "It's just that he won't do it."

Homework assignments are missing, his work is sloppy, and he's more immature than his classmates. The other kids laugh at his jokes but don't include him in their games. The truth is, Cara and Brian have known about his behavior problem since he was in third grade.

They could attempt to solve the problem in several ways. First, they could blame each other. Brian might say, "You spoil him. Quit doing everything for him. You're making things worse."

She could respond, "If I don't sit there with him and make him do his homework, he'll do nothing at all. You don't know what he's really like. You're never home. Besides, you let him walk all over you. It's your fault he's like he is, not mine."

Blame doesn't usually change things, so if they respond this way the problem could go on for a long time. Cara could continue her nightly vigils at the kitchen table, feeding her son his school-work until the walls could repeat the answers, all behind her husband's back. Brian could continue to work late, and when he is home, silently defend his son against his mother's control.

Instead of blame, they could try to solve the problem through self-denial: Cara could suppress her worry about Terry and promise to save her assistance for final exams. But she would probably walk the halls of her house, anxious and afraid, terrified that her son might be put back a grade. If he was, it would be Brian's fault for denying their son help.

Brian could suppress his fatherly perception that Terry needed to do things on his own and instead agree to back his wife. He might even discipline Terry for failing at school, but this would probably happen either half-heartedly or with such force that his son would be stunned and hurt, wondering what had gotten into his father.

Either way, both parents would still be withdrawn or overly in-volved with their son, and eventually they would turn hostile to each other. When an agreement is based on self-denial no one gets what he or she really wants. When it's time to carry out the deci-sion, the players are likely to do so lethargically, instead of having the energy that comes from doing what comes from the heart.

Suppose they reject blame and self-denial, and look for a third way? What then?

They might try managing conflict with resonance.

They would begin by respecting their own perceptions—with-out diluting them with blame or self-denial.

Brian might say, "I love my son, and I believe that giving him the room to be self-reliant would help."

Cara could say, "I love him, too, but I believe he needs more discipline to succeed."

Using double vision, Brian would set his own perceptions aside for a moment and be open to Cara's thinking. Then it's more likely he would understand that in her desperate effort to help, she was trying too much. He might realize that she needs his help.

As Cara listens she would understand that Brian's "do it by yourself" attitude is his way of trying to get their son to be self-reliant. Brian might also be right about some things. But his way isn't working either. He also needs her help.

They talk until they understand that they can't effectively parent their son if they're also fighting over him. They both care, and they both must find a way to be on the same side.

Brian says, "I don't want to be the absent father, but I fall into it when things aren't going well between us. I want to be involved. I want him to achieve, but I don't want us to have to do it for him."

Cara says, "It's good to hear you say you want to be involved. I'm tired of being the homework police. I'm tired of us fighting over him. I need you. But I also know he needs more discipline."

Now they brainstorm together. "What if we set a study period, one hour a night? He has to sit in his room, no stereo, no phone calls. But we won't check his assignments or even go into his room. Whatever he does in that hour is up to him. I'll come home early a couple nights a week. You won't have to be the bad guy. If he studies, fine. If he stares at the walls, well there's nothing we can do. He's the one who has to take the ball and run with it."

She builds on what he has said. "How about taking fifteen minutes after the hour is over to review what he has done and to help him with any problems? Maybe if we both do it, he'll know we mean business—and we both care about him."

They go back and forth until they come up with a synthesis that works for both of them. It's better than what they began with because it includes both her desire to give Terry help and his desire to let Terry make his own decisions. They feel good about their plan, energized, and ready to make it work. They both get what they want and strengthen their relationship at the same time.

Making Resonance Work for You

It's not always easy, but when you resolve conflicts with the goal of resonance in mind, you feel both free and close. Certain steps, such as the ones Brian and Cara followed, make it possible.

Step one: Use your resonant intention to avoid hostility.

Anger is a feeling that occurs when you feel threatened. You can't avoid that. But you can avoid the hostility that's used to demean another person. When you're in conversation, one trick is to tag anything that feels demeaning and try to stop it. Some couples use the simple phrase, "I feel attacked," to tag hostility in arguments and reduce it. If this works, you're less likely to turn your own anger into a hostile counterattack.

Step two: Manage hostility by taking a break from each other.

Just because you're in an argument doesn't mean you have to continue at that time. However, after you've had a chance to cool off, you must return to the discussion. Otherwise, this conflict will be added to the larger store of avoided conflict collected over the years and will simmer away dangerously. If you simply take some time out, you have an opportunity to examine your anger and reach for a deeper understanding of yourself.

Step three: Allow yourself to feel your anger.

Don't be afraid of your anger, and don't express it too quickly to your partner. Instead, trace that anger back inside yourself. Sometimes that's difficult because anger is such a powerful emotion—at its peak, hands shake, faces flush, and minds close—and it's easy to be afraid of it. To use anger well, you can't succumb to that fear. Ask yourself, "What's this all about?" Open your mind to your inner voice. Do you hear a little child who's warding off the feeling of being controlled? Do you hear an outraged adolescent who thinks that being wrong is the same as being rejected? Here's an opportunity for greater insight into your past, so you can understand why certain comments trigger anger.

Step four: Separating out "I" from "you."

There may be a difference between what "I" perceive and "you" intend. For example, a woman I know said to her husband, "I'm angry that you're late. I was scared that you were in an accident." Note that she talked about what she felt and left out any comment about what her husband intended. It's true he may have been late because he wanted to frighten her, but his lateness may have had nothing to do with her—she just doesn't know. But she can ask.

And a man I know said to his girlfriend, "I'm mad that you didn't stop at the store for me, even after I called to remind you. When that happens, I feel unloved."

Note that he simply talked about what he felt and didn't make any comment about what his lover intended. Again, there was more than one possibility: She truly might not have cared enough to remember or she simply could have had other priorities—he just doesn't know. But he can ask.

Talking about what you perceive and asking about what the other intends are the two sides of healthy anger. Of course, you may find that the other person did indeed intend to harm you, but jumping to that conclusion too quickly can trigger exactly what you fear. What we believe isn't always what other people intend.

Ask yourself: Do I really believe that my partner has the best of intentions? We can't share power until we share trust. If you doubt your partner has your best interests at heart, then both of you have to make the time to deal with the basic issues of trust.

Often mistrust is the result of early life experiences, of past hurts. Understanding how mistrust emerges in each of you is the beginning of the work necessary to draw a distinction between your past and your present relationship.

Step five: Make use of your double vision.

To use double vision, begin by stating your separate perceptions. This is your understanding of the conflict and a statement of your basic needs. Then stay open as you listen to your partner. Mirror his or her words. Make at least one understanding statement.

In an argument, for instance, a man might say, "Golf is important to me. I need to get out on the green with my friends. I can understand that you look forward to being with me on the weekends, and I know that when I make plans to golf with my friends it cuts into the time we can spend together."

The woman might say, "When you play on Saturday and Sunday, it doesn't leave time for us. I need to do things together on weekends. I realize you've waited all year for golf season and that you haven't seen a lot of your friends since we moved in together."

Then they might brainstorm a solution that feels right to both of them. They must learn how to look for the new synthesis, the creative approach that is the product of both/and thinking. That means they must listen to each other's ideas and use their creativity to build on them. The couple in the struggle over golf might come up with any number of solutions. He might spend somewhat less time on the green with friends; she might learn to play golf herself, so they can play together at times. Or, they might both take up tennis. It all depends on what feels good to them. This is what resonant couples do when they face conflict.

Using anger well isn't easy. But it's worth it.

It is possible for most of us to use our resonant intention to avoid hostility. We can use our felt sense to identify our anger and our inner voices to understand where it comes from. If we add to that the technique of double vision, we're more likely to come up with solutions that work for both of us. Then we can create the kind of relationship in which we can be fully ourselves and share ourselves fully with someone else.

An Anger Workshop

Test your skills at avoiding hostility while still expressing your anger with the following exercise. Answer these questions and compare them to the answers below.

Difficult Situations

1. Your lover didn't get you a birthday gift, and the first thought that jumps to your mind is, "He must not care about me." What will you say?

2. She calls you lazy when you lie down on the couch after dinner to watch TV. How do you respond?

3. You're out to dinner with friends, when he says, jokingly, that you're the worst money manager he's ever known—you can't add two plus two. What do you do?

4. She says, "You never have been, and never will be, a good parent." You ask, "Do you really mean that?" She says she really does. You feel like counterattacking with "I'm a better parent than you'll ever be because . . . " What do you say?

Resonant Responses

1. Express your own feeling about the missing birthday gift and ask what happened. "I feel hurt that you didn't get me a present. How come you didn't?" Remember, what you

perceive and what your partner intends may be two different things.

2. "Lazy" is often used as a hostile put-down. Tag it by responding, "That feels like an attack. It makes me want to attack back. Can you stop?"

3. If you have a moment of privacy during the evening or the next day, tag the hostility in his statement about your money sense. Try to agree to avoid such hostility—especially when you're with other people. You might say, "That was a put-down. I've probably done the same to you, but I don't want that in our relationship, either by you or by me. Can we agree to try not to?"

4. Take time out. "Let's talk about this after dinner. I'm too angry right now."

It's easy to make our relationships into battlefields. I've known many people who have. Fear is the prime motivator. Avoidance fuels the process because we close down and so don't learn how to manage our fear. Add to this a dose of blame and an attempt to find some safety through control, and hostilities are very likely to break out.

Creativity and self-awareness are vital to using anger well. Listen to your thoughts to understand where the anger comes from. Use your felt sense to face your fear and to understand that fear comes and goes, which makes it less likely that fear will get in the way. Doing these things, you'll be able to work with your partner to avoid hostility and to create the kind of relationship in which you both feel safe.

The Gender Trap

> And perhaps the sexes are more related than we
> think, and the greatest renewal in the world
> perhaps consists in this, that man and maid, freed
> from all false feeling and aversion will seek each
> other not as opposites, but as brother and sister,
> as neighbors, and will come together as
> human beings.
> —Rainer Maria Rilke, *Letters to a Young Poet*

Josh was driving Betty to her friend's surprise birthday party when he made a wrong turn.

"We're lost," Betty announced.

Josh, staring silently ahead, never even took his foot off the gas pedal.

A few moments later she broke the silence again. "Look! There's an open gas station ahead on the right. Why don't you stop and ask for directions?"

"I'm not lost," he said. "Don't worry, I'll get you there on time."

Five more minutes passed. By now Betty was chewing on her cuticles. She looked at Josh in disgust. "We are lost, but your male ego won't let you admit it. I'll never understand men. Why can't you ask for directions?"

Like many other men, Josh likes the challenge of finding his own way in the physical world, and it can seem unnecessary or even like a failure to ask for help. Like many other women, Betty tends to rely on relationships to find her way through life, so asking for help seems like the natural thing to do. Each of these people thought the other's approach was wrong.

A week later, they had another round of the same problem. Betty was talking about whether she should go through with her plan to undergo surgery for an old knee injury.

"I hate the thought of going under the knife," she told him, worried. "You never can tell what will happen. Maybe I should get another opinion. What do you think?"

Trying hard to be patient, Josh said, "I don't know why you torture yourself with all this worry. Be logical. You've already gotten two opinions. Stop being so emotional about it. Go in and get it over with already."

Betty knew she would begin to cry if she tried to explain how rejected and dismissed she felt. Without saying another word, she went upstairs and called her friend Sally for a good long talk. Josh was hurt and confused by her abrupt retreat. He had tried to help. He thought he would never understand his wife.

Once again, these two confused each other. Josh interpreted Betty's first comment as a request for help in deciding whether or not to have surgery. Like many other men, he prided himself on his capacity to bring logic to bear on a problem. But Betty didn't want him to solve anything at all—all she wanted was to share her worry. Like many other women, she wanted to feel close and connected when a difficult issue arose.

We Are Different

It's true. Biology as well as thousands of years of experience and learning have shaped us so that each sex talks, acts, argues, and makes love somewhat differently. Some experts say this is because we're brought up in distinctly different ways, almost as though we live in separate cultures—sometimes almost separate planets.

These differences wouldn't be a problem if we could simply notice them and leave it at that. The trouble is that most human beings have a knack for doing the hierarchical two-step: First we notice differences, and then we rank them better and worse. For instance, Betty noticed that Josh never asked for help with directions, but then she put him (and all men) down for it. In her mind, hers was the better way.

Josh did the same two-step. He noticed that Betty was worrying about her upcoming surgery but had no patience for such "illogical" thinking. His was the better way. Difference became a matter of better or worse.

In my clinical experience men and women often speak in negative generalizations about each other. Men often say that women are engulfing, sexually unresponsive, too sensitive, moody, and very absorbed in personal appearance. And women often say that men are unemotional, condescending, and thoughtless of other people's needs.

They also make positive generalizations: Women are nurturing, warm, sensitive, loving; men are strong, logical, protective.

These generalizations aren't about the sexual identity of people (their bodies), but rather about their gender identity (what it is to live in that male or female body). While our sexual identity is determined only by biology, we develop our gender identity through learning.

Whether negative or positive, all of these generalizations about gender are a problem because they are prescriptions for how to live. For instance, women are "supposed" to be more nurturing than men, and men more courageous than women. In fact, we train boys and girls to follow these prescriptions. Boys are discouraged from cradling dolls, and girls are discouraged from climbing trees. This kind of gender training begins early in life, continues in school, and via the media, throughout adulthood.

The training is so powerful that at times it does indeed seem as if we come from different planets.

The Greek philosopher Plato imagined that the first human beings were more complete than we are now: round, with four hands, four feet, one head, and two faces looking opposite ways. Because of their form, love was unnecessary. They were also so terrible in their "might and strength" that they eventually attacked the gods themselves. Zeus became so offended he considered annihilating the whole race. But after talking with the other gods, he decided instead to cut each one in two. That's why, Plato explained, we exist as we do; we are half of our original selves, "flat fishes" or "indentures" of the full beings we once were. Zeus's punishment also made love necessary.

While we might not describe it the way Plato did, we live a rendition of this story today. We have to find our other halves to feel complete. Still worse, we often consider one half (male or female) to be better than the other. The result is a war between the sexes, and as we shall see, that war also takes place inside each of us.

A Divided Psyche

The gender problem can be visualized in the shape of a barbell, with all the male characteristics at one end and all the female characteristics at the other end. Each end has a distinct and separate set of prescriptions, and there is no confusion, no overlap.

At first it seems as if the bar in the middle acts as a barrier, and so neither gender is "tainted" by the other. The only way to know the other end of the barbell is to know a member of the other sex.

But that's not the way it is for people. Actually, the entire gender barbell is inside each person's psyche—with one side marked positive, acceptable, right and the other marked negative, shameful, wrong.

A man must follow the prescriptions marked positive for males while diligently avoiding those marked negative. A woman must do the reverse. If we slip up, others are quick to notice. But even without their comments, we tend to know ourselves and may feel badly or shamed by the transgression.

In this way, we become stamped-out copies of our gender and avoid the mix of human characteristics, the range of choices, that is more likely to lead to the development of authentic, individual human beings.

These gender prescriptions also do damage to our relationships. Judging certain gender traits better or worse makes it very difficult to connect with a member of the other sex.

Hierarchical thinking is at the hub of the gender problem—and there is evidence that this was not always the case. In *The Chalice and the Blade,* the archaeologist Riane Eisler, a student of prehistoric human cultures, reports on another relationship model between the sexes. Weaving together evidence from religion, history, and art, she suggests that there was a time in our ancient pastoral history when men and women were connected by what she calls a *partnership* model, an egalitarian association marked by cooperative relationships. She notes that it is possible we can evolve to another rendition of this partnership model so that people of each gender can advance their own development without having to limit the development of people of the other gender.

Love and Gender

▪ Anthony and Teresa

Anthony is a powerfully built stonemason, a man's man—one who thrives in the company of other men. Teresa is an earth mother. With her mother and sister nearby, and her four young children, she is a cheerful homebody.

One morning Anthony awakened with a slight fever. Teresa suggested he stay home, but he refused. Driving was difficult because the roads were slippery. His head felt heavy, and it was hard for him to focus. Just as he began to think that he should turn around, another car skidded into his lane. His reaction time was too slow, and he woke up in the hospital with a concussion and a severely herniated disc.

After his stay in the hospital, Anthony was ordered by his doctors to go home and rest in bed for six weeks. At the beginning, he was in too much pain to think about much else, but eventually he became more and more irritable. Teresa received the brunt of it.

Soon he was telling her what to do with the house and the kids. "You don't know how to organize things," he said. "The house is a mess. There's stuff everywhere. You should clean up instead of talking on the phone with your sister. You let the kids walk all over you. They don't listen. They do only what they want to do."

Teresa felt it was futile to explain that he really didn't know what it was like to run a house and take care of four children under the age of eight. But she began to feel more and more incompetent as he railed against her. By the time they came in for counseling, she was furious at him.

Like many other merged couples, Teresa and Anthony lived at either ends of the gender barbell. They had male and female ideas about how to manage illness, how to love, and how to rear the next generation. And since the tendency toward hierarchy is triggered by such extreme differences, without knowing it, they each attacked the other's way of life.

Teresa usually felt like a competent mother and homemaker—she got plenty of affirmation from her mother and sister about that. When Anthony began to complain, however, she began to see herself through his male eyes, and she didn't like what she saw. The mess in the house became evidence of her incompetence rather than the natural outcome of rearing young children. The children's behavior became wild and bad rather than spirited and normal.

Anthony had his own problems. He usually considered himself strong and independent, while Teresa was weak and dependent. But lying in bed, he worried that he was becoming more like her. When Teresa tried to comfort him, he got truly frightened.

If a man is ashamed and disdainful of personal qualities he thinks of as female, it's likely he will be even more disdainful of those qualities in his partner. That's what happened to this couple. As Anthony lay in bed, he became contemptuous of his own "weakness." When he thought he saw that same quality in Teresa, he couldn't contain his rage.

■ Tom and Laura

Laura grew up in a dying town where her father, who worked in a paper goods factory, barely worked enough hours each week to make ends meet. At home, he sat in front of the television set. Her mother would often take Laura aside and pour out her bitterness. "The trouble with your father is that he's weak—no backbone. Don't ever get caught with a man like that. Make enough money to support yourself. Be independent."

With the help of a scholarship, Laura escaped her hometown and her parents' unhappy marriage. She graduated near the top of her class and joined a public relations firm immediately after college. She met Tom at a conference. He was the comptroller of a successful electronics firm. The suit and tie, the attache case, fit the male image she was looking for. He made good money, and more important, he had plans for making even more. Laura had visions of an equal relationship, with both partners carrying their own weight.

Tom was persistent in his pursuit of her. He called every day and made sure they saw each other every weekend. Laura was captivated by his self-assured behavior—it matched hers. After a six-week, whirlwind romance, they were married.

By the time they came in for counseling, Laura realized that she had been fooled, and more important, she had fooled herself.

Mesmerized by her fantasy of a successful man, she didn't notice what she called Tom's lack of drive, his hesitation, his passivity. Too late, she realized that he didn't really want to advance at work, and his salary didn't cover his half of the expenses. He wasn't even interested in fixing the cars or repairing the house, which had been bought with her money. This was not a fair trade.

As it turned out, Laura was repeating her mother's experience. She was living with a man she couldn't respect. Worse still, Tom complained that she was too aggressive, too career oriented. Even the way she was able to balance the checkbook to the last penny irritated him.

The truth is, Tom had always worried that he wasn't masculine enough, and when Laura began to complain about just that, his self-esteem plummeted. Laura had the same problem. She always feared that she wasn't feminine enough, and as a result of his complaints, her self-esteem suffered, too.

They saw their other-gender behavior in disapproving ways. His quiet, contemplative nature became "passive," and her dynamic qualities became "aggressive." They needed tremendous energy to manage their shame—energy that would have been better spent exploring their positive potential, regardless of gender prescriptions.

The Gender Challenge

Think for a moment. Is it important to you that others see you as feminine or masculine? Do you have trouble accepting women who are aggressive or have other qualities you think of as "manly"? Do you find yourself uncomfortable around men who are sensitive, or those who aren't concerned with getting ahead and staying ahead? How comfortable do you feel with your gender identity?

If these gender issues are troubling or confusing, you're not alone. These issues are old and pervasive, and many people have struggled with them. As far back as the middle of the nineteenth century, ferment over the rigidity of women's roles and their lack of freedom seethed. Over the ensuing 150 years, many books have been written on the subject.

John Stuart Mill, a remarkable man and a prominent nineteenth-century philosopher, condemned the Victorian morality that considered helplessness and dependency the pinnacle of the female character. He denounced social institutions that evoked cruelty in husbands and provided no redress for wives—laws that allowed a wife to be subject to domestic slavery without even the right to compel her master to sell her. He also fervently believed that reform in our institutions would cause the "apparent" differences between the sexes to disappear.

We now know that significant social reform did come over the next 150 years, but markedly different prescriptions for each gender persisted. Role behavior may be less rigid today, and women and men may be able to understand each other better than they did a hundred years ago, but both sexes are still bound by gender stereotypes.

Contemporary feminists believe that this is primarily due to the way the sexes are enculturated. While we come to life with differences in temperament, we are taught our gender roles. The result, according to sociologist Jessie Bernard, is that men and women behave as though they live in different cultures. This makes mutual understanding a matter of cross-cultural interpretation.

In this same tradition, psychologist Carol Gilligan has explored male and female differences in moral behavior. And linguist Deborah Tannen has studied how men and women use language differently.

Today, more and more of us are challenging all the conditioning that makes people try to squeeze themselves into traditional roles. But even those of us who feel quite liberated find that gender prescriptions seep into our relationships. A woman recently told me, "I got really irritated when he couldn't look under the hood and tell me what was wrong with my car. What kind of man can't find his way around an engine?"

A man confided, "I can't see myself married to her. When I talk to her about my career, she's not interested. When I give her advice about hers, she never takes it."

Another man said, "She gave me advice in bed—do it softer, not there, over here, like this—and it drove me nuts. I want a real woman, not a choreographer."

Wanting the man you love to understand how to fix the car or be a good lover is not wrong. There's no problem with wanting the woman you live with to be a sensitive listener. The problem comes when we expect another person to be a certain way simply because of their gender, or when we feel we have to be something we aren't, acting in a way that isn't fully ourselves because we think we have to conform to traditional gender roles.

It never works. If a man feels he has to be strong and is driven to perform, he may lose a sense of himself because his energies go toward denying whatever else inside him doesn't fit this picture. If a woman hides her sharp intelligence to protect him and avoids being what he might think of as aggressive in bed, she may feel empty even when he tells her how much he loves her. Neither are able to reveal themselves to the other. Neither are able to love and be loved for who they truly are.

We don't have to turn our backs on femininity or masculinity to get out of this trap. We need a new way of thinking about gender that takes us inside our bodies and outside of tradition.

We Are All Unique and Human

Imagine all our human characteristics spread out like a rainbow of colors, so that identity becomes a mixture of hues. A man or woman may have a little more of the color called competition, another a little more of the color called cooperation. Now it doesn't matter what gender prescriptions are. When you can explore all the colors of this rainbow, you become the best that you can be and create the safety needed for your partner to do the same.

I know a strong, solidly built mother of two who is a carpenter by trade and a sociologist by training. She walks, talks, and looks like a laborer, thinks like a highly educated person, and holds her baby like a loving woman. She is a woman who has been free (and proud) to choose a variety of hues—and in the mixture, she is unique.

As a therapist, I'm often impressed by how similar our basic wants and needs are. Underneath all our defensiveness, everyone I work with, male or female, wants to feel safe and trusted and free to become themselves. Most of us want to be competent and have the kind of closeness that leads toward intimacy. We may go about it differently, but we all want love.

One woman discovered this truth when her husband lost his job. He seemed so sure of himself as an executive of a large corporation; so capable, so strong, so different from her. All that changed after a few months of unemployment, when he began to feel unsure of himself, at a loss for knowing which way to turn, and in need of considerable emotional support. It reminded her of what she went through when she put her career on hold for a few years after the birth of a baby. Gender prescriptions allow us to forget that men and women are more alike than they are different.

Learning to Value Differences

At our very best, gender does play a part in who we are. Men and women are different but not sharply so. And neither is better nor worse. When a father nurtures his child, his protective behavior has a certain male quality, quite different from that of his wife. His child responds to that. When a woman manages a work group, her problem solving has a certain female quality, different from a man in the same position. The work group responds to that. Gender makes us different, but we also have the same human needs.

What if we learned to value the differences between the sexes instead of demeaning those differences? What if we knew that while each of us has a male or a female body, all of us have a mix of both masculine and feminine gender characteristics?

Accepting and valuing all our human characteristics—whether they be labeled "female" or "male"—is extremely important. First of all, our personal development is inhibited if we disown a part of ourselves because it's "wrong." I know many women who dislike themselves because they're "aggressive" or "outspoken." And I know many men who hide themselves because they aren't "aggressive" or "outspoken" enough.

Second, valuing the different parts of ourselves is important in a relationship. We can only love in another what we can love in ourselves. We can only love what we don't feel afraid of. A man who disowns his emotional side may also reject a woman who's emotional, telling himself that she's too "needy" but fearing that he might detect some of that emotion in himself. A woman who dismisses abstract logic as "callous" and "the wrong approach to life" might rage at her husband if he tries to rationally think through a problem she feels emotional about. She might fear the confusion that sometimes comes with strong emotion and believe she doesn't have the capacity to think clearly.

Only when we know we have the potential for all the human capacities in ourselves—for physical and emotional work, for nurturing children and exploring the world, for rational thought and intuition—will these qualities be available to us. Celebrating these characteristics in ourselves can help us celebrate them in those we love. Resonance takes place when we value differences and sense the human needs we share in common.

However, we can't forget that gender prescriptions are powerful determinants of personality for all of us; they are integrated into the basic stuff of our being. Besides, there's no antigender pill that anyone can take. A couple in search of resonance must begin by heightening their awareness of gender prescriptions and how they can diminish self-esteem and make mutual respect less likely.

If we reject these gender prescriptions as a guide to development, and use our talents and interests instead, we're more likely to emerge as authentic individuals. If we also create relationships that nurture each person's development, that authenticity is even more likely.

This is a process, not a single event you can make happen. I can't give you ten easy steps. However, I can suggest some guidelines that can help you face the gender challenge on the way to resonance.

Becoming the Best That You Can Be

Use your capacity to focus inside.

Listen to your inner voice as you think of the gender "oughts" in your life. Some of them will fit you well, others will feel wrong. Value your hidden desires. If you do, you are more likely to make choices based on your interests and special gifts. That's a big step in personal development. As a woman, gender prescriptions say you are likely to be the following.

Someone who likes to nurture rather than be nurtured. Is it hard to give yourself the present of personal time, or to ask someone else to help make your life easier? Or are you a woman who doesn't follow the norm?

Someone who is more of a "feeler" than a "thinker." Do you want to further explore your intuition (perhaps through an art form) or do you want to try your hand at rational thinking (perhaps by studying macroeconomics)?

Someone who, in mixed gender groups, allows others to interrupt and override what you say. Do you think of it as a personal problem? Perhaps instead it's built into the relationship between the sexes.

Someone who is more of a collaborator rather than a competitor. Does your capacity to cooperate suit you, or do you have secret yearnings to come out the winner?

Someone who would rather talk about people rather than about mechanics, sports, or business. Or maybe you don't follow the norm.

As a man, gender prescriptions say you are likely to be one of these types.

Someone who is more interested in your career than in child care. Does the generalization fit, or do you want more consistent and close contact with children? Perhaps you want both.

Someone who would rather confront the issues, perhaps get into a good fight, rather than "making nice." Does being competitive suit you better than trying to get people to cooperate? Or do you not follow the norm?

Someone who is more interested in time for yourself rather than getting involved in putting the baby to bed. Would you rather read the paper or cook a dessert for dinner? Do you have the internal freedom to choose?

Someone who moves toward problem solving rather than delving into emotion. Can you switch from one to another?

Someone who, when making love, moves quickly toward sexual intercourse. Or do you enjoy prolonged talk and cuddling? Do you like both at different times?

Some people criticize those who try to free themselves of gender prescriptions. Others criticize those who follow them. For this reason, it's important to draw boundaries—an imaginary line that keeps others out and protects you from their criticism. Then you can focus inside and risk stretching toward behaviors you enjoy or find challenging, regardless of whether they're labeled "male" or "female," and you can discover aspects of yourself that have been hidden, fostering traits you never knew you had.

"Ever since Jasmine started preschool, people have started asking me when I'm going to go back to work," a client told me. "When I tell them I'm not planning to, they look at me like I don't have goals or something. I'm happy being a mother, being a wife. I've worked. It was no big deal."

Following the traditional expectations of your gender is not a problem so long as you don't feel controlled by them. Whenever you let the "oughts" and "shoulds" of anyone else restrict your freedom, whenever old notions keep you from being yourself, opportunities for resonance are blocked. Instead, let your special gifts or the interests that engage you lead the way.

Use your capacity for double vision.

Double vision will help you value your partner and, perhaps, a hidden part of yourself. This was how one woman used double vision to understand her husband.

She: Why are you so worried about losing your job? With my income we'll be all right. Besides, you'll find another.

He: You don't understand. I can't take the idea of being out of work calmly. Without a paycheck and an office to go to, I feel like I'll lose part of my reason for being—even if we don't need the money.

She: I'm beginning to think that even though I'm successful at work, I'm not as tied to it as you are. I often catch myself thinking that I would like to spend more time with the kids. We're different. Even so, I'm not the traditional mother, with all the time and energy I put into work.

Both men and women view their work as part of their identity, but women often have other priorities as well. Children often take precedence. The preceding woman managed to take part in both worlds.

This was how a stepfather used double vision to understand, and make room for, his wife's loyalty to her children.

He: Why can't you let those kids lead their own lives? You're always worrying about them. They come first in your life, rather than me.

She: They do come first. I feel they've needed more from me since the divorce. I'm sorry you feel hurt by that.

He: It's hard for me to understand why I can't be the one who comes first, just as I make you first. I guess that's part of being a mother.

To live well with a member of the other gender one needs double vision. First, we need a capacity for deeply felt empathy. As Jose Ortega y Gasset describes in *On Love,* "We need a peculiar kind of initial curiosity which is much more integral, deep-rooted, and broad than mere curiosity about things. . . . We must be vitally curious about humanity, and more concretely about the individual as a living totality."

Second, double vision is based on the capacity to maintain a separate voice or to have a will of one's own. Maurice Friedman, in "The Basis of Buber's Ethics," explains that when one person meets another "he does not lose his standpoint, his center. If he sees through the eyes of the other . . . he does not lose his own eyes. He realizes himself as an I, a person, through going out again and again to meet the other." The other person, or the thou, "teaches you to meet others and to hold your ground when you meet them" (pp. 196–97). Both aspects of double vision are important when people of different genders, and therefore with a different socialization, are living together.

Gender differences do exist, and it's better for people to understand them and make room for them, rather than labeling them right or wrong, or expecting that men and women be exactly the same. Sometimes we can dip into both gender roles to get the right fit.

One couple, Sylvia and William, have become adept at this. They use double vision to explore their separate approaches to life. Sylvia tries to learn from William about leadership and addressing groups, and William tries to learn from Sylvia about relating intimately, simply enjoying the pleasure of the experience without having to get things done. William knows that he's exploring the male as well as the female visions of life, and Sylvia knows that she's doing the same. Neither fears losing their separate senses of self. They are free to learn about the other gender in their psyches.

Be proud of who you are.

Clearly affirm both your so-called male and female characteristics and the range of your development. Doing so, you will also feel closer to the person you love.

He: I've got a soft, nurturing side to me, and that's all right.
She: I've got a tough, hard as nails place inside me, and that's all right.
He: I feel taken care of when she makes money.
She: I feel taken care of when he makes food.

Affirming both sides of the gender polarity inside you is empowering. It dispels the notion that you must be bound by gender prescriptions and validates the reality that we all have the same basic human needs.

George was a man who spent years trying to avoid depending on his wife, Shelly. Even the thought of it made him feel as if he was less of a man. He never looked to her for support either financially or emotionally. He never put his head in her lap or cried when times were rough. And he felt very alone.

Then he had an affair, and the marriage almost died. With this new woman, he allowed himself to be more needful, more openly human. His marriage seemed barren by comparison. When he and his wife first came into couples counseling, his wife was too hurt and angry to hear about anything but his disloyalty. It took time, but George stayed with her, and slowly she heard that he was more aware of his need for her. Soon he was proclaiming his dependency, even his vulnerability. His wife responded by feeling closer to him, and the marriage took a leap forward.

Use your resonant intention with courage.

People need courage and clear, conscious intention to make choices that rely on talent as a guide for growth.

For example, Seth and Sharon are a couple who waited until they were in their late thirties to have a child. After the birth of their daughter, Emily, Sharon took only six weeks maternity leave and then unhappily returned to work.

With tears in her eyes, Sharon said, "I know I have to work full time, but I miss Emily. And I'm tired all the time. I get up at 5:30 in the morning, nurse the baby, and then rush out to work. Luckily, my time in the lab is flexible, so I can come home once during the day for an hour. But almost as soon as I walk in the door at night, it's time to eat, clean up, and get Emily ready for bed.

"My mother's making things worse. She calls every day, mostly at the lab, and tells me I'm harming the baby by leaving her with a sitter. I know she only wants the best, but my stomach gets into knots when I hear her voice."

In therapy, Seth and Sharon developed their vision of a family by answering concrete questions: What kind of time do you want to devote to taking care of Emily? Which of the many parenting tasks do you think are especially important? How close do you want to be with Emily? How close do you want your partner to be with Emily? What balance between career and home feels right? The answers to these questions helped them envision the future. Then they could use their intention to change their life.

First, they created boundaries to give them more space to bring reality closer to their vision. Sharon spoke to her mother about the difficult time she was having juggling work and home and asked her to help out by not calling at work with criticisms. With some difficulty, her mother rose to the occasion. And then Seth and Sharon used their intention to shape their special approach to parenting.

"If I could have just what I wanted," Sharon mused, "I'd work half days. It would give me a chance to be mother as well as researcher. I'm going to speak to the head of my department and see if it's possible. Maybe we can live on less money for a while."

Seth said, "I've been so caught up in making money that I didn't see the truth: I really don't want to miss so much of Emily's early years. I can work less time. I want to make fathering a priority for now. I'm not going to take any new clients for the next couple of months. Then I'll see how we feel."

In these ways, they shaped a life they both wanted to live.

Catch yourself in the way you think about gender—and then experiment in your mind with other possibilities. We often repeat the mistakes of others, but there's always an opportunity for change.

I end this chapter with a personal experience—one that illustrates how Bob and I try to use our intention to go beyond gender prescriptions.

Recently, we bought a small boat because we both wanted to enjoy being at the edge of the ocean. Beyond that, our desires for the boat were different. My dream was to watch sunsets and explore the marsh. Bob wanted to fish.

Once we got our nineteen-foot beauty, I quickly learned that "she" was mechanically complicated; it took skill to maintain her. It even took skill to steer her through the maze of markers down at the New Jersey shore. Not surprisingly, Bob, being male, was more willing and able (though also anxious) to take on these challenges. If we followed this typical gender scenario, we both realized that he would become more involved with the inner workings of the boat and more comfortable finding his way on the water. Without planning to, he would become the "captain" of the boat while I would become a passive, less-involved passenger. Neither of us wanted this outcome.

We had several alternatives: I could recognize my limitations and give up my interest in the boat and the marshes. Bob would continue to enjoy the boat with friends, adding another male experience to his life—a clear benefit. But we wouldn't have the shared experience.

We could also sell the boat.

None of these alternatives felt right to us. Talking about it together, I decided I would learn how to run the boat—how to back her up, how to take the wind into account when docking, how to read and remember the placement of the markers. And I would try to learn about the engine. Given that Bob feels more comfort in this world, he offered to help me, and I accepted his offer.

If this plan works, we'll both get what we want: We'll both know the boat. He will fish, and I will sit quietly in the marshes early on summer mornings listening for birds and watching the movement of the wind on the water. It may also be that I will fish and he will listen for birds. We'll see.

That's the kind of gender work that makes the peak experiences of resonance more likely.

CHAPTER 9

Feeling the Beat

If a man does not keep pace with his companions,
perhaps it is because he hears a different drummer.
—Henry David Thoreau, *Walden*

It's Tuesday night, a slow night at the city's premier health club, a two-acre status showcase that boasts a membership of nine thousand young professionals, some looking to improve their bodies, some merely looking.

A man and a woman sit two seats away from each other at the upstairs bar, a popular spot strategically placed between the locker rooms. They sip their drinks slowly and, as if by chance, turn toward each other. They nod and glance into each other's eyes and then quickly turn back to their drinks. Moments later they repeat the sequence, only this time he adds a tentative hello before turning back to his drink.

The third time their eyes meet, he leans toward her while nodding intensely, but she seems hesitant. Moving still closer, he drums his fingers excitedly, but she leans away. As he tries to introduce himself, she averts her glance. After awhile, he stands up, excuses himself, and leaves.

What happened? The answer depends on who tells the story. He said she was too passive. She thought he was too pushy.

From my perspective they failed to connect because they were out of step, out of the rhythm that's essential to intimacy.

Your Interactive Rhythm

We think of rhythm as something indispensable in music, but it's also essential in relationships. We create a beat as we interact with each other, responding to words and movements. Looked at from this perspective, relating is a dance. When we're in rhythm we feel great together. Out of rhythm, we have difficulty talking about the weather.

Research tells us that the potential for creating interactive rhythms is inborn, but much like talking or walking, it needs practice. Babies practice by moving in relation to their mothers' bodies and in beat to the language being spoken. In the early stage of a relationship, and without awareness, couples practice their rhythm as they walk, talk, eat, and make love. Some people have trouble establishing a satisfying beat; perhaps they can only create it after a few drinks. Others feel comfortable only when they dominate.

Think about your relationship for a moment. Do you feel connected? Or, is most of your life spent watching the clock and meeting the work deadlines, so that you never seem to get together? Do you complain that you don't spend enough time together while your partner talks about the need for more "space"? Are you annoyed that he or she makes so many demands on your time? Have you ever felt that even when you're together, you're lonely?

The trouble may be in your interactive beat. When you talk, do you create a back and forth rhythm that feels satisfying? Can you work or make love together so that you feel connected but not overwhelmed? It's a special kind of rhythm that people thrive on, a pulsing relationship between separateness and togetherness. This chapter takes a look at what inhibits couples from finding that beat.

Although some of our best moments with a partner seem to happen with no warning or planning, you'll find that there are a number of things you and your lover can do to make those moments more likely to happen.

▪ *Jean and Richard: No Time for Love*

When the alarm rings at five in the morning, Jean, a pediatrician, forces herself out of bed to do thirty minutes of exercise. By seven-thirty, she's dressed, showered, and seeing her first young patient at the hospital. On Monday and Wednesday mornings, she works at a clinic. On Tuesday, Thursday, and Friday mornings, she's in her own office seeing children at twelve-minute intervals until one in the afternoon. Afternoons follow a similar pattern except for the days she teaches at a local medical school, the preparation for which requires at least two evenings a week. Only on weekends does she have any "free" time.

Richard, her husband, owns several successful men's clothing stores across the city. He gets up at six each morning, jogs several miles, and then dresses for work. By eight he's at the office. Several nights a week he stays at a store until ten at night. Other evenings he devotes to racquetball or basketball; Saturday is for golf—and networking for business opportunities.

When they first came in to see me, Jean's complaint was that Richard never seemed to have a moment for her. "I can't understand why he won't come home early at least one night during the week. Most evenings I'm in bed when he finally arrives, so we never see each other."

Richard was annoyed. "You're so involved in your own work that you rarely have time for anything else, and yet you talk as though I'm the problem. You want to spend some time together? How about Monday night?"

"Come on, Richard, you know that's my night to prepare for my class."

"Tuesday night?"

"Don't you play racquetball Tuesday nights?" she asked.

"Yes, but I'm free by nine. We could go out for a late night dinner."

"By nine I'm too tired. I see at least twenty-four patients in a day."

They both looked at me, as if to say, "See? It's impossible."

The media has given couples like Richard and Jean their own acronym: DINS, "double income, no sex." Work, work-related socializing, sports, and school all add up to no time for conversation, let alone intimacy.

Clock Time Versus Intimate Time

We live our lives in relation to several different time pieces— each of which fits different human needs. In clock time, work and responsibilities take precedence; we use wristwatches and appointment books, keeping track of whether the minutes are being spent to achieve our goals. In intimate time, relationships take precedence; objectives, plans, or purposes are secondary. The pleasure of connection is primary. We might plant a garden, take a walk, or go out to dinner. We pattern our behavior in relation to one another, and only secondarily in relation to any outside measure of time.

If you're like most people, however, you can probably understand the feeling of being pressured by clock time—the rhythm of our urban culture. Its pace is rapid, a march of very brief moments filled with many, often too many, activities. This kind of time is signaled by sharp and intense markers, like the sound of the morning alarm or the roar of traffic getting into town. Time means money, and that topic generates much of the stress we carry around. All this leaves little opportunity for impulse, improvisation, or relationship—for the kind of time that holds the promise of resonance.

There's nothing absolute about our way of measuring clock time. It actually changes from culture to culture: The pace of life in rural Mexico or Brazil is slower, the markers less intense. In many cultures time isn't like our march of undifferentiated moments, instead it's cyclical—time goes round and round from planting to harvest, from birth to death. This pace makes for more awareness of our connection to previous and future generations.

Our culture is different from others in that we think of each unit of time as infinitely divisible, down to trillionths of a second. By making electronic time that functions in these unimaginably brief moments, we stretch time so we can do more in each moment spent. But even the old-fashioned mechanical clock is a relatively new invention, and only with it can we have half-hour appointments or ten-minute coffee breaks.

Clearly, our mechanical and electrical clocks are not natural or even necessary. Clock time, however, is one of the major inhibitors of intimacy—especially for energetic, success-oriented people like Richard and Jean.

As Richard and Jean discussed the importance of their careers, and their attachment to clock time, I suggested the possibility that they lived by the clock not only to make money and be successful but also to avoid intimate time. Perhaps they were having trouble finding a satisfying interactive beat together.

To see if this was true, they decided to set some boundaries around their work and allow for intimate time, and then see how well it went. Following this suggestion, Richard and Jean decided to spend Friday nights together. To do so, they would have to let nothing else interfere.

According to Jean, the experiment went downhill fast. She said, "The first Friday night was good, and the second was okay. But Richard didn't show up for the third. He said he forgot."

Richard's version was different. He said, "The first Friday, Jean spent the whole evening worrying out loud about work. I could see that the second Friday was going to be more of the same, so I told her that she was missing the whole idea, which was to get away from work. Then I got a lecture on how I don't listen to her. The truth is, she's so lost in her own problems that she never listens to me."

Richard and Jean found they were competing for each other's attention. She wanted him to focus on her, and he wanted the reverse. When they didn't get what they wanted, Jean kept on talking and Richard withdrew. This pattern was so unsatisfying—and the interactive beat so poor—that they avoided spending intimate time with each other. Clock time was more satisfying.

In counseling, Jean became aware of how much she needed Richard's attention, and how frightened she was of losing it. Richard discovered how much despair he felt at never getting the attention he needed. They both understood they were turning to work because their needs for attention and appreciation were being met in that arena.

Richard and Jean were caught in clock time in part because they weren't doing well in intimate time but also because they, like most of us, never thought there were alternative time pieces they could use consciously to help them. All work and no play isn't inevitable. It can be a choice.

In therapy, they began to use double vision to sense each other's tempo. They listened closely and shared their concerns. When they resumed their Friday nights together, it was with the intention to change. Sometimes they overcame the fear of being ignored; at other times that fear prevailed. Sometimes talk flowed freely; at other times it became stilted. Yet they kept at it until they got better at letting the focus of attention move from him to her and from her to him. They were learning how to be together in intimate time.

Personal Time Versus Intimate Time

Personal time is measured by clocks that are built into our very bodies. There are several types. One is tied to the seasons. Maybe, for you, spring is a time of renewed energy and winter a time to slow down. Perhaps winter is a time of depression for your partner, with anxiety, irritability, an inability to concentrate, and a loss of interest in life. Psychiatrists now have a name for this more serious problem; they call it SAD—Seasonal Affective Disorder.

Another body clock is tied to the daily rising and setting of the sun—your sleep pattern, body temperature, pulse rates, and even your capacity for memory change during a twenty-four-hour day. You might be a night person, which means your pattern of sleep and activity is reversed; you're more awake in the middle of the night than you are in the morning.

Each of us has a unique cycle of activity and rest. Maybe you think fast, move fast, and can decide exactly what you want in ten seconds. Perhaps you're quiet and deliberate, and your decisions must be well thought out and researched. Or, your life is a roller coaster, up one moment, down the next. Whatever description comes closest, you have your own rhythm or beat.

People have trouble when their internal rhythms get in the way of the demands of clock time. Doing shift work or traveling across time zones, you can fall out of phase with the daily cycles of light and dark and not feel well. You can also have trouble if your in-

ternal rhythm is different from your partner's, which can get in
the way of intimate time. You may move slowly while your partner moves quickly. Your partner may be at peak performance
early in the day while you perform better at night. If you happen
to be in a relationship with someone whose biological clocks run
at a pace different than yours, trouble brews.

Sometimes your clocks are so different that simply being around
each other sets your teeth on edge.

"It takes her so long to order in a restaurant I want to shake
her."

"He's so hyper, he makes me nervous."

"She talks so fast, no one can get a word in."

"I get sleepy at eleven, but she wants to be up until all hours."

▪ Ronald and Marie: When People Hear the Beat of Different Drummers

Ronald and Marie were both systems analysts working in the
same department of a large corporation. Theirs was an office romance—brief, exciting, and troublesome.

Problems began when they were asked to work together to develop a computer program that was supposed to be on-line within
twenty-five days. Seven days into the project, Ronald was late
with some figures needed to test phase one of the program. Marie
asked where they were, and he told her, "I'm so busy trying to
stay on top of everyday problems that I haven't had a second to
think this through."

Marie, upset about the lateness, remained hopeful. "I know
he'll get the job done in time," she thought. "He's a wizard, once
he gets down to work."

On day fifteen, Ronald began to focus on the job, but by this
time Marie was so upset she could barely cooperate. "We'll never
finish in time," she told him. "Don't you understand that my rep-
utation is on the line as much as yours?"

"You're in a panic over this, and it's unnecessary," he argued. "I've finished phase one, and I'll finish the rest. I do my best work under pressure."

They finally produced the computer program just two hours before the deadline, but by then their relationship was over. Their internal timers were set to run at different paces. Marie's was synchronized to work steadily, but Ronald's wasn't. Yet even when they were alone, they irritated each other. They couldn't function as colleagues or lovers. Nor did they want to make the investment to explore their time problem and try to change it.

■ *Dorothy and Michael: Night Person/Day Person—*
The Great Divide

Two people do better with time if they are aware of and respect their differences. Given our tendency to create hierarchies of better and worse people, however, it's all too easy to judge someone according to how fast or slow their personal clocks tick. We might even find ourselves rejecting the other or striving toward an unfair balance that makes that person feel dominated. If we can set aside these judgments, we're more likely to find a mutual rhythm that works.

The challenge begins with awareness. What are your personal rhythms? Can you "own" and respect them? Listening to your own internal clock leads to a greater awareness of your personal needs, and that's important in any relationship.

Dorothy and Michael, for example, were a couple who never went to bed at the same hour—a pattern that caused havoc in their sex life. Absorbed in their hectic work and family lives, they avoided the problem for years.

Michael, a marketing consultant, had trouble concentrating during much of the day. He "woke up" about three in the afternoon and did his most productive work after ten at night. Just as

Dorothy was about to go to sleep, he settled himself in front of the computer. For many years this pattern worked. He was so intent on success, and she was so exhausted at night after a day with the children, neither seriously complained about the absence of intimate time—or their infrequent sex.

As the children grew, trouble exploded. Dorothy began to need more from Michael, and she began to complain about his work hours. In turn, Michael blamed Dorothy for their limited sex life. He was hurt and resentful that she had "spent years being too tired." But their internal clocks had been set so that intimate time was rare, and now their challenge was to leap over the divide between day and night people.

In therapy, they spent hours clearing away the judgment and blame that often emerges when people have very different internal rhythms. Once they had done this, they were ready to pay attention to their own internal clocks. I asked them both to trace the rhythms of their energy as it ebbed and flowed through the day by tracking when they felt awake and when they felt tired.

Michael wasn't surprised to find that he had trouble getting up in the mornings, but he was surprised to realize that he also had a down time after dinner. He sometimes even felt like taking a nap before he settled in for his night's work.

I asked Dorothy to pay particular attention to when her body actually felt ready for sleep. She always thought she had to close her eyes by ten o'clock. She learned that if she went to bed before eleven, it was likely she would wake up during the night. Her sleep rhythms had changed, and she didn't need as much sleep as when she was younger.

With this kind of awareness, their day/night patterns began to loosen around the edges. Michael tried getting into bed around ten in the evening with Dorothy, so they could spent some time talking, even holding each other, but I asked them to avoid all the complexity that goes with sex for a while. That way, it would be easier to work on their time problem. When Dorothy was ready for sleep, and he felt more rested, he got up and continued his evening's work.

Michael described the results of this experiment, saying, "That hour in bed during the early evening is time out for me, and I've begun to enjoy it. We cuddle and talk, and I know I don't have to stay. I actually look forward to it."

Several years later, when they came in for a checkup, he added, "The remarkable thing is that I've slowly trained myself to go to sleep earlier. Now we tend to get into bed between eleven and twelve, and we're making love more often. We're even having breakfast together in the mornings, and that's really a change. Of course, I sometimes stay up late if I have work to do, or if I need some time alone. I guess we're more flexible now."

Michael and Dorothy were able to move away from hurt and resentment, from judgment and blame, and shift their sleep pattern to allow for intimate time.

Now Time and the Peak Experiences of Resonance

Some people call it "living in the present," others call it "stopped time." Artists look to now time for inspiration, mystics to transcend everyday life, and people in trouble experience it as healing. Now time offers a slice of life beyond our personal concerns; we can move out of our separate skins and know the larger whole. It's the feeling of being both separate and connected—and that's what resonance is about.

You can prepare yourself for now time by letting go of purpose and immersing yourself in some part of life, perhaps art, nature, or sports. You'll know it's happening when a surge of awe or joy swells within your body.

Couples can also experience now time if they immerse themselves in such activities together. That means letting go of purpose—be it finishing a task, disciplining a child, or achieving an orgasm.

You can prepare for these peak experiences by fostering your sense of safety with each other. That means dealing with issues of power, managing conflict, and exploring the restrictions of gender. Along with this, you can consciously set the conditions for now time. Skip the workout, leave the dishes, flip on the baby monitor. Explore your interactive beat. And if something always happens to interfere, ask yourself: Might we be avoiding intimacy? Why? What happens when we're together? What do I feel? What does my partner feel? How can we prepare ourselves for letting go and feeling safe?

You can't force those special resonant moments to happen, but you can manage time so they're more likely.

Take a closer look at the way you live in time.

Talk about the mix you and your partner have created between clock time and intimate time. Would you like more of one than the other? Is intimate time difficult because your partner's "beat" dominates? Do you try to dominate his or hers? Realize that you have the power to shape your time to fit your needs. See if there's a mutual desire to create interactive time.

Take a closer look at whether you live in relation to your internal rhythms—in personal time.

Perhaps you need more free time or quiet time. Maybe you need more time for personal pursuits.

Realize that not everyone's internal clock ticks at the same rate. Give each other the freedom to explore and value his or her personal beat. A man who functions at a slower rate than others might think of himself as dull or even lazy. A woman who functions at a faster rate might think of herself as manic or pushy. It helps to become more aware of your special beat because you can give it the value it deserves. You can also use this knowledge to create a better interactive beat with your partner.

Give each other the freedom to say no to intimate time.

You can only say yes fully if you can also say no. You can never be certain that your partner will want to be in intimate time when you want to be. Even the secretion of the hormones that triggers sexual desire can be different for each of us. For this reason, asking for intimate time necessarily means risking rejection. And this is easier to do if you and your partner have already agreed beforehand that saying no to intimate time is okay.

Remember to pay attention to transitions from one type of time to another.

Whether it be the discomfort of jumping from the dryness of the air into the wetness of a swimming pool or of going from purposeful clock time to the nonpurposeful experience of intimate time, transitions are challenging. Making matters worse, we often interpret the time a partner needs for transition as a rejection, and this isn't usually so. The swimmer might hesitate before jumping in but still thoroughly enjoy the water, and the person who is in clock time may enjoy intimacy—once he or she switches time pieces. What is required of the person doing the asking is a little patience.

If a man is busily involved and his lover reaches out for intimate time, he would do well to recognize his need for a transition and ask for it. And his lover would do well to realize that there isn't any on/off switch for intimacy. When one person asks for intimate time and the other has to say no, the squeeze of a hand, an appreciative glance, and a "thank-you-for-asking" go a long way toward softening the feeling of rejection that usually arises.

Create the setting for now time.

Couples in a resonant relationship seek out those special moments when time itself seems to stop. They treasure the moments when they are so immersed in the present, perhaps deeply absorbed in music or looking deeply into each other's eyes, that they almost forget about breathing. Each person feels clear and strong, and also part of the union. Sometimes he or she knows that their union is also part of the larger mysterious whole.

Here are some examples of the settings you can create to ready yourselves for now time.

Create your own rituals—planned moments of significance that ready us for something special. Early morning walks, monthly "get-away" weekends, or the yearly "return to nature" vacation can offer the opportunity to sense the stillness behind time's never-ceasing motion.

Bob and I have an old farmhouse tucked deep in the woods of northeastern Pennsylvania that we go to every four or five weeks to take in the quiet. For us, it's a ritual. Just turning off the car after the ride down the long dirt road that leads to the house releases the tensions from my body. And if we're very fortunate, the hollow sound of a hermit thrush or the sight of a doe will welcome us.

Music and art are pathways to now time. We think the special feeling of certain rhythmic sounds is created by the music we hear, but that's not quite the case. While these rhythmic sounds seem to originate in the music, they actually originate in us, and the music releases them. It's the musician's genius to be so deeply in touch with our basic rhythms that his or her composition resonates deep inside us.

The same is true for the visual arts—the relations of shapes to each other, color against color resonating inside us, releasing our appreciation.

What kind of music do you enjoy listening to together? Do you enjoy dancing? Do you make time for this part of life?

Active participation in a sport can also be a path to now time.
When you no longer have to think about the skill involved in a
sport, when your mind is still and your body engaged, you may
know one of those moments when time stands still.

One couple regularly plays tennis together, sometimes pairing
up for a doubles game. Well matched, they move their bodies in
relation to each other and through the medium of the ball. The
dance is highly satisfying. When their minds and bodies are finely
tuned and their concentration clear, they feel deeply connected.

Spend time together without having a purpose. I know a couple
who feel that sense of oneness with each other while walking the
streets at dawn when the city is awakening. All they do is walk
and feel the stirring of life around them—a solitary woman slowly
walking her dog, a night watchman making his way home. This
couple is open to the spiraling beat, the gathering of energy that
emerges when many people begin their day separately and together.

This, too, can be a backdrop for resonance.

Another couple regularly take a couple of glasses of wine, a
blanket, and a tape player outside in the evenings and lie down on
their back lawn. Sometimes they share stories; at other times
they're silent. But most of all, they tune out the memory of their
busy day. Recently, at a moment when everything was in place,
they experienced a moment of oneness with the universe as they
stared at the stars above.

People who are in resonance move into each other's lives with
deep respect. They create a rhythm that sings connection and hon-
ors separateness. That rhythm is a mystery built into our world,
whether in the flow of a flock of birds, beautiful music, or two
human beings walking down a street together.

Resonant Sex

... and then I asked him with my eyes to ask again yes
and then he asked me would I yes ... and drew him
down to me so he could feel my breasts all perfume yes
and his heart was going like mad and yes I said yes I
will Yes.   —James Joyce, *Ulysses*

There is something elemental, even mysterious, about resonant sex. It's a way of momentarily transcending the loneliness of our separate selves. Skin no longer feels like a boundary keeping us apart but rather like a doorway that leads to intimacy. Going through that doorway, separate selves fade and two become one; returning, we feel separate and somehow enlarged.

There is a play and rhythm that two people in resonance create, as well as solo performances. It might happen like this: Welcoming the beauty of her lover's nude body, feeling his heat warm her skin along the long stretch where they almost touch, the woman welcomes her desire. Slowly, her hand moves to trace the line of his chin, the sweep of his soft lips. Gently, she pulls the hair that threads his chest. Somewhere along the way his earlobes become intriguing, so she kisses them and jokingly asks whether the right one feels different from the left. He wrinkles his forehead in mock concentration, explaining that the question was one he had never considered, and suggests they do some research. Looking into each other's eyes, they laugh.

As the excitement grows, she's like the conductor of an orchestra, her motions surging and waning in anticipation of his response. Then it seems as if he's the conductor, and she answers to his eyes, his arms, his kisses. Ultimately, they no longer know that they have separate bodies and so become one splendid instrument creating music that becomes a backdrop for their lives.

Feeling safe, they pay full attention to the ebb and flow of their excitement. Feeling free, they're spontaneous, playful. When the moment is over, they return, deeply enhanced, to their separate selves.

I know some couples who have resonant sex often, and I know many others who never do. This chapter describes how struggles over power, traditional gender role expectations, and clock time stand in the way and how couples in search of resonance deal with these problems. If a couple can create a safe enough environment, they can explore their separate sexual needs, which, if they value them, can lead to resonance.

Our Unloved Sexual Selves

Each of us has the potential for resonant sexuality. It often happens spontaneously in the romantic rush of a new relationship. That's when couples are intrigued instead of judgmental; curious rather than bored. They are pleased, even proud of the sexual gifts they can give each other.

Why does this simple human pleasure disappear in so many relationships? Why do we think the loss is natural?

One reason is shame. Many people do not trust the feelings that accompany good sex because they seem out of control and dangerous. Sexual shame begins early in life. Especially in adolescence, when arousal and desire seem most unpredictable and uncontainable, protective, well-meaning parents often communicate that all sexual thoughts and behaviors are wrong, bad, and frightening.

In the worst cases, shame and fear occur because of sexual abuse—when an adult makes a child the object of his or her desire. In other cases, the rejection of erotic sensations, passed down through the generations, simply continues habitually, unquestioned. Whatever the reason, there are many young people who feel guilty simply because they feel sexual. The outcome can be adult sexuality choreographed like a well-rehearsed minuet— "proper" or even "bad" but devoid of open and loving erotic feeling.

A woman of thirty-two admitted, "I never take my clothes off in front of my husband. I don't even like to use the word 'sex.' The whole thing makes me feel dirty."

A man who denies himself sexual thoughts said, "I'm embarrassed because I have these erotic fantasies. I try to stop myself. I even force myself to think about something else, but it happens anyway. I know it isn't right."

All this guilt and shame is a problem because sexual feelings and thoughts are a kind of energy, a food, and denying them is like denying hunger. With a tremendous will we might manage to do it, but we soon feel irritable, deprived, and devoid of vitality. Some people don't even know they're starving.

A second reason good sex disappears is that almost everything else comes first. By the time most couples get around to sex, they're in bed after a busy day and in need of sleep. Stretches of interactive time are essential to the health of a relationship, and without it sexual pleasure will remain minimal. "Only peasants make love at night," English aristocrats used to say.

Third, good sex disappears because we don't accept our aging. Our bodies are changing every day. The rapidity and intensity of sexual response is markedly different at age twenty, thirty-five, or forty-five. And yet many of us think, and the media suggests, that we should function in bed as if we were always eighteen years old. The truth is, sex at an older age isn't better or worse, it's different.

A forty-year-old man said, "I used to get an erection just by looking at a woman, and now it seems to take forever. When my wife and I are making love, I'm so nervous about it, I can barely pay attention. There must be something wrong with me."

This man and his wife began to have better sex when they let themselves explore the slower, more subtle and cooperative sexuality that takes place in middle age. An erection may take longer to achieve, women may need more time to feel excited, but each of these changes offers new opportunities for exploring who we are sexually.

Ask yourself how fear and shame and self-criticism might be poisoning your sexual relationship. Can you and your partner talk openly about your aging, and how that affects what you need from each other? Does your management of time interfere?

Blaming Our Partners for Problems of Our Own

Bill and Joan hadn't had sex for eight months when they first came to see me.

He: I guess I've never been the touchy-feely type. We don't have that kind of relationship. But we only make love once or twice a year. That's her fault—either she doesn't have the time, or she's too tired. To tell the truth, I don't feel the urge very much anymore.

She: Between his nighttime job, my work, and the demands of the kids, we barely see each other. It doesn't usually bother me that we don't make love very much. Besides, I don't think he's a very sexual person.

This is an example of the mysterious process by which partners become reflections of one another. Bill admits that he's not "the touchy-feely type," but then he quickly makes Joan responsible for the lack of sex in their relationship. Joan admits that she's not that interested in sex, but then she makes Dan responsible by saying he's not "a very sexual person."

What's going on here? Psychotherapists call it projective identification—when we place, or project, on someone else a disavowed or dissociated personal characteristic. Not only do we come to believe these characteristics exist in our partner, but through suggestions we encourage him or her to behave as if they did! Then it's easy to blame the other person, rather than hold ourselves responsible for our own troublesome personality characteristics.

In therapy, after Bill could talk about his own sexual troubles, he had less need to blame Joan for them. After Joan stopped accepting Bill's projection, she could talk more openly, and with desire, about her own sexual needs. Then they were on the way to better sex. It was never perfect. They didn't make love more than once or twice a month. But they did hold each other more frequently, and they could talk about their desires.

Sex is a rich medium for confusion. When we feel shame or fear, we are likely to try to project those emotions on our partner. If we do, it's likely that our personal problem, perhaps shyness or lack of desire, will actually show up in our partner's behavior. In bed, we are often least our separate selves and most merged with our partners.

All this gets further complicated by gender prescriptions. Many men, for instance, won't ask for a hug because they think it's too feminine. If a man happens to crave a hug, he's likely to dismiss the craving and project it onto his partner. Then he can vicariously enjoy his wife's desire for a hug—or get angry at her for not wanting to be close. It seems easier that way, but it's at a cost to his own sexual development.

The same is true for women. Many women won't initiate sex because they believe it's a male prerogative. If a woman happens to be assertive, she hides the desire to initiate even from herself. It's easier to make that a characteristic of her male partner. Then she can vicariously enjoy his sexual persistence—or get angry at him for not pursuing her. But this is at a cost to her own sexual development.

Gender prescriptions lead us to reject parts of our sexual selves, and projective identification leads us to expect those rejected parts in the other—or to blame him or her if we don't get what we want, like a hug or an initiation of sex. Then we're likely to express a range of critical, angry feelings, overtly toward the other and covertly toward ourselves.

Sex, Power, and Gender Role

Sex gets confused with power. More accurately, the mix of the need to control the other and rigid gender roles denies us the safety we need for resonant sex. For instance, for a man to live out the male gender prescriptions of the virile stud, it is expected that sexual pleasure include a desire for control over the woman. Initiating sex is considered good and waiting for a woman to initiate sex is considered bad. Infidelity is almost a requirement and loyalty a sign of weakness. For the man, the role is often used as a mask for self-doubt or sexual disinterest. In the worst cases, the man will become abusive and treat the woman as an object who can be forced to do what he wants. What a poisonous brew!

However, many women expect this behavior from their men. They vicariously enjoy the freedom and power that comes with the male role. Unfortunately, this deprives them of their own freedom and power.

For instance, if a woman never needs to pursue a lover and risk rejection, she protects herself from the anxiety associated with the pursuit. She assumes the waiting role and expects the man to initiate. She enjoys being the focus of desire and yet doesn't own her own desire. Most troublesome of all, even if she dislikes being the "object" of desire, through her passivity, she enables the male sexual pressure she really doesn't want.

The female counterpart to the stud is the prostitute—the woman who flaunts her sexuality, accommodates the man, uses sex as a tool for personal gain, but whose eroticism is rarely loving. While the male image of the stud is generally acceptable, the female counterpart is seen with shame and even disgust, a symbol of the negative attitude we bring to sex. Often men project this image onto women. In this way, the man can make the woman responsible for sexuality he finds personally unacceptable, while seeing his own sexuality as acceptable—though this represents a double standard.

Renee and Benjamin, a couple who came to see me when Renee became depressed, lived a rendition of these roles within the four walls of their home. Though for several years Renee had rarely felt sexual, she always tried to act and look appealing, even if she didn't feel like being close. Late one afternoon, Renee was lying on her bed feeling restless and lonely when she heard Benjamin's key in the front door. Throwing on a revealingly tight sweater, she ran downstairs and gave him a hello kiss even before he took off his coat. She described what happened next.

> He responded by grabbing for my left breast. I must admit that I cringed. He could have at least said hello. Soon I realized that he wanted sex before dinner. I really wasn't interested, but I couldn't say no. He would have been angry.
>
> I knew the routine even before we started. He likes me to be his expensive call girl, stripping right in front of him. So I pulled my

sweater over my head slowly, kicked off my shoes, and peeled off my jeans. I'm embarrassed to admit this, but he likes me to brush my hair in front of the mirror so he can see my breasts bob and my neck arch.

He pulled me toward him quickly. It was one of those times when he didn't treat me like a person but like some kind of sexual aid. Anyway, he entered quickly, came quickly, and didn't ask if I was satisfied. But that really didn't matter to me. To tell you the truth, I wasn't feeling particularly sexual. I just wanted him to finish quickly. I knew my six-year-old son would be home soon, and I had to cook the chicken or we wouldn't have dinner.

Benjamin wasn't happy either. The pleasure of the sexual experience quickly faded. Something was missing, but he didn't know what it was.

These two were living the sexual fantasy of the powerful man and the available woman. Renee dressed for her man, waited for him, and had sex for him. She didn't know her own erotic desires or how to make her own sexual choices. In the end, she felt empty and depressed.

You might imagine that Benjamin had more sexual freedom, but he was held by chains of another sort. Studs need sex to feel alive and potent, but they're often trapped in behavior that is too self-serving, too unrelated to their lover's to get the validating response they need. Benjamin needed Renee desperately, but she was closed to him.

The fact is that many people feel sexually aroused by this mixture of disengagement, power, and sex. The theme is so common that it seems natural, almost necessary, but it actually takes considerable training—often in early family life and always through the many images of sexual victimization that pervade our media. Female models frequently look as if they're victims, sometimes as if they've just been beaten up, and male models don't look much better. We're intrigued by indications of abuse. It's a powerful theme in our culture.

As Renee and Benjamin worked in couples therapy, she talked about how it felt to take part in their sexual game. "I used to think it was exciting to be with such a strong man. I actually felt safer, more open to my own sexual feelings because he was forcing me. But over the years I began to feel used. Now I know I can't let this happen."

When Benjamin heard this, he looked toward me and rather bluntly said, "Don't let her fool you. She may talk as though she doesn't like the way we have sex, but I know she loves it."

In truth, the mixture of power and sex fascinated them both. It gave Benjamin a sense of potency, and it protected Renee from the responsibility of making personal sexual choices.

Many people are mesmerized by this sexual fantasy. It's an embodiment of the extremes of gender role and power. To believe that it really represents how men and women are, however, is damaging to each person and the safety of a union. More constructively, adults can, if they like, play with this all-too-human theme, acting it out as a self-conscious fantasy. You and your partner can pretend that one person is in control, always remembering that he or she really isn't. You can even reverse roles. This is the wonder of play.

Less extremely, many people feel powerless in bed because they never develop their own sexual voices. Either they don't know enough about their own sexual response to know what they want, or they can't ask their partner to participate. The result is often avoidance, indirect talk, or outright manipulation. Here are some examples:

- The woman who pretends a wild abandon she doesn't really feel: "If I scream and act like he's an incredible lover, maybe he won't leave and look for someone else."
- The woman who fakes an orgasm to "get it over with." "If I pretend to finish quickly, so will he, then I can get back to what I was doing."

• The man who has an affair so he can have the "security" of multiple partners, then lies about it. "How can you question my loyalty? You know I have late night meetings."

• The woman who demeans her partner's sexuality through sarcasm and ridicule: "Only an animal would want that!"

• The man who tries to be one-up by threatening to walk out: "You leave me no choice. If you can't meet my needs, there are plenty of women who will."

• The woman who uses her power covertly by "having a headache": "I don't feel that well tonight."

A more subtle example of control occurs when people can't develop a mutually satisfying sexual rhythm. Instead, one person's needs take priority, and the couple misses the opportunity for union. In the following example, the man's needs are more important.

> He likes to have a "quickie" before he goes to sleep at night. I've begun to realize that sex is like a sleeping pill for him; it helps him relax. It's a routine—as soon as the light goes out, he reaches for me. Sometimes I give in just to get to sleep, but at other times we fight about it. He's a very selfish lover, and then he has the nerve to say that I'm the problem because I don't like sex as much as he does!

Sometimes it's the woman whose needs are more important.

> She got up earlier than I did and went out to jog. By the time she came back, my mind was filled with all that I had to do that day. I really wanted to get up, but she came back into bed and wanted sex. If I said no, she would get hurt and sulk. It wasn't worth the three days of silence, so I tried to perform. But it didn't work—I couldn't get an erection. She finally left the bed frustrated and angry, and I felt like a failure. We spent the rest of the day avoiding each other.

Another problem occurs when one person's preferred rhythm is faster than another's.

She takes a long time to get excited, so I try to hold back my own excitement while caressing her. Then I guess when the moment is right to enter her. Sometimes I'm right, and we have a great time. Often I'm wrong—and I come too quickly and leave her frustrated.

In all these examples one person's needs dominate, and the other, without an effective sexual voice of their own, is left behind. When we follow rigid ideas about gender and get caught in the pitfalls of control power, when we have sex to please someone else, or when we allow another person more sexual freedom than we allow ourselves, we close the door to resonant sex. Is there an escape from these control problems? Can you understand that your partner has separate needs? Is there room for two separate individuals in your bed?

Four Varieties of Sex

Sex is a small word but it covers a lot of territory. Let's begin this search for resonance in bed by identifying the different varieties of pleasure.

■ Personal Sex

Personal sex is the realm of erotic thoughts and feelings—of self-pleasuring. Many people avoid personal sex because it triggers shame and guilt. Others enjoy pleasure of many kinds—the sun's heat on the nude body, an erotic fantasy, the intensity and release of masturbation. All this is beyond the eyes and ears of the world and doesn't hurt anyone.

■ Flirtatious Sex

Flirtatious sex is the play between people who are enjoying the first traces of erotic feeling. It's a testing of mutual interest. If the sexual feeling isn't reciprocated, the flirtation is over almost as soon as it begins. If both partners enjoy it, they might move on to a relationship that holds opportunities for other kinds of sex.

Some people never flirt because they fear the fuller sexual feelings they might unleash. Others take the risk without thinking about it. Still others consciously decide whether the person and the context are right. If so, they communicate a little of their erotic feelings and then see what happens. Like any other mode of sex, flirting is a pleasure in itself, and there's no need for it to lead anywhere.

■ Sensual Sex

Sensual sex is the realm of touch, from the affectionate hug to the slow, erotic caress. It doesn't include contact with the more highly erotic parts of the body, such as the breasts, the genitals, or the buttocks. Sensual sex is enjoyable if the context and the person are right, if both people feel safe and are able to give and receive with pleasure.

Some people avoid sensual sex out of discomfort with their bodies or because they've never learned to enjoy it. Women often stay away from it to avoid intercourse: Alice moves to the other side of the couch when her husband sits down. She does like to be touched, but she doesn't always want to have intercourse. Sometimes her husband does want to have intercourse, and he reads her behavior as a rejection—all this without any words being spoken. At other times, intercourse is not on his mind at all, but there they sit, at opposite ends of the couch.

Men often consider sensual sex a tease if it doesn't lead to intercourse. "All she wants to do is kiss and hold each other. She gets me all excited and then says no. It's not fair." A couple with this conflict is struggling over the kind of closeness they want—and often no one is talking about it.

Everyone does better if they talk about what they want. Sensual sex is a realm all its own, a pleasure in itself that can be enjoyed if both people want it.

▪ *Genital Sex*

Genital sex involves the most erotic parts of the body. Men more often than women mistakenly think it's synonymous with all sex, and thus limit their pleasure. Also, genital sex is where many people feel the most fear and shame. A man might worry about the size of his penis or whether he moves to climax too fast or too slowly. A woman might worry about the size of her breasts or whether erotic thoughts are appropriate. With enough excitement, however, most people can break through these feelings and enjoy the pleasure of genital sex.

It's important, then, when searching for resonance, to intentionally shape your life so that sex can be enjoyed in its many varieties.

Reaching for Resonant Sex

Chances are, you have experienced moments of resonant sex in your lifetime—moments when you felt clear and focused on your own excitement, and at the same time, united with your lover. These are the peak experiences of sex that you remember to this day. Fortunately, you can consciously prepare yourself, and prepare your relationship, so that these moments occur frequently.

Focus inside to achieve resonant sex.

The search for good sex can begin by looking inside yourself, by focusing on your own erotic feelings, paying attention to where in your body sexual feelings begin, how they spread, and when they are most intense. Do this alone, in privacy. Enhance it with sensual music and erotica of many kinds. Toy with fantasies—what they are isn't as important as the fact that you have them.

Here's a single woman's experience:

> Once I realized how much time I was spending at work, and how little I was enjoying life, I decided that things had to change. Then it occurred to me that I've been waiting for men to give me pleasure rather than giving it to myself. So now I devote Thursday evenings to myself. When I come home from work, I turn off the phone, put on some good music, take a really hot bath, and focus on my own pleasure. Sometimes I read a novel, sometimes I decide to sleep, and at other times I give myself an orgasm. I just pay attention to my own pleasure.

Focusing inside is also important when you're in a relationship. Flirting can only happen if you feel erotic. Passionate sensual or genital sex is only possible if you can feel your body even as you interact.

A man recently told me:

> I've always been a guy who wanted to please a woman in bed. In fact, I could only get excited if she was excited, so I would wait for her to get ready, try to anticipate her needs, and stifle my own excitement until she was ready. I got so worried about pleasing my new girlfriend, Mary, that I forgot about myself, and I started to have trouble maintaining an erection. Now, when I feel excited I try to go with it, not forgetting Mary but being willing to stay with my own feelings and leading the way. I checked it out with her. She says it's all right with her, and she'll tell me if it isn't.

Using double vision to find resonant sex.

Double vision gives you an opportunity to pay attention to your own excitement while being in touch with your partner. Kevin and Sharon, recently married, battled over when was the right time to have sex until they learned to use their double vision.

Kevin said, "I used to think Sharon should be just like me, and I like sex at night. I would get angry at her for saying no to me before we went to sleep, and then wanting me to perform for her when we got up. But I've begun to realize that there's room for more than one way."

Sharon said, "I'm learning that there are times when I can follow his lead and enjoy myself. The other night we saw a sexy movie, and we rushed right into bed when we came home. I'm all for it, if we also do it my way."

Fantasy and play can enhance your pleasure.

When it comes to sex, you need to pay attention to boundaries. Locking the bedroom door keeps children out; unplugging the telephone and turning off the television keep the world out. Both are essential to the pleasures of the body.

There's another kind of boundary that separates sexual thoughts or fantasy from sexual behavior. Without that boundary, people are more likely to believe that a sexual thought necessarily leads to action. Many a married woman feels guilty for having a sexual feeling when in the presence of an attractive man, and many a married man feels disloyal if he has even a fleeting image of sex with another woman. It's as though the thoughts themselves are disloyal.

But there's a clear difference between an erotic thought and a sexual act, and one doesn't necessarily follow the other. If you remember the boundary, you can think what you want, as long as you filter your thoughts through an ethic of caring before taking action. Louise learned to do just that, and it freed her to enjoy her own erotic fantasies.

"I used to keep my sexual fantasies about other men to myself because I worried that Henry would be upset. Recently, I began sharing some of them, and he loves it."

We have as much freedom as we can allow ourselves in the realm of thought. Sexual fantasies can be as wildly imaginative as anyone cares to make them, as long as the boundary between fantasy and reality is clear—and if the fantasies are shared, as long as the two lovers feel turned on by them. Each couple is different; each sexual relationship needs to be tailor-made. There's no one right way.

Similarly free is the realm of play, in which we act as if our actions are real when we know they're not. We make such games safe by granting each other the right to stop them anytime it feels uncomfortable. Sex and fantasy and play go well together.

One woman told me:

> Jim and I share a sexual fantasy. He likes to think of me as a woman he has just picked up, and I like to imagine that I'm waiting to be picked up. Last week I put on a sexy dress and went downtown to a prearranged meeting place—a bar. And when he came in, we acted as if we didn't know each other. He "picked me up," and then we took a cab to a local motel. We even talked in front of the cabby as if we were two strangers out to spend the night together. It was good fun.

Resonant Sex and the Real World

Many people say to me, "This is all fine, and I can see where listening to my partner, being more open and playful and less judgmental, would be good for both of us. But, this is the real world. Will this really lead to resonance?"

▪ Matthew and Julie

I assure you it can. Matthew and Julie are a good example of how resonant skills work in the "real" world. Three years before they met, Matthew's first wife died, while Julie had been separated from her first husband for two years.

Matthew's sexual relationship with his first wife had floundered as she became sick with cancer, but the truth is that they were never a very sexual couple. Somehow, when evening time came, his wife was too involved with the children, and Matthew was too involved with work. They never talked about their lack of sex being a problem.

Julie's first husband had difficulty having and maintaining an erection. They tried many approaches to the difficulty, and ultimately discovered that he really didn't want to be that close to her. They never found their way to the safety that good sex requires.

Matthew and Julie had a very different sexual relationship. Matthew couldn't get enough of Julie. It was as though he was making up for lost time. He would wake up in the morning with a desire for sex, and with night came more desire. They would spend long weekend afternoons in bed making love, sleeping, and making love again.

At first, it felt great, but eventually Julie began to feel controlled by his seemingly ever-present need. As she began to say no, they began to argue.

"I won't go through another drought," Matthew said. "Sex is too important to me. How can you do this to me? You know what I've been through!"

"I won't have sex when I don't feel like it," Julie responded. "And I don't feel like it as much as you do. One thing I learned in my first marriage is that it doesn't work to forget about myself."

There was no simple right and wrong side to their dilemma; each person had a different sexual rhythm. How could they be true to themselves and yet satisfy each other?

In a close relationship, you can try to get your needs met in one of three ways: by force, through negotiation, or by searching for a solution that meets each person's deeper needs. Taking the last approach, you avoid either/or answers and search for both/and answers. This is the way to resonance.

In therapy, Matthew and Julie began by exploring their separate sexual needs. Matthew's fear of losing another sexual partner kept him on the edge of panic. Would Julie disappear sexually like his first wife did? Julie worried about getting caught in the trap of trying to please a man who can never be satisfied. That got her back up. In this relationship she had little opportunity to know her own desire or initiate sex herself.

One day, they were ready to use their double vision to try to solve the problem. First, they listened closely to each other and affirmed each person's right to separate sexual feelings. They also kept their own needs in mind.

Julie said, "I understand your worry, and please understand that I don't want to be like your first wife and reject you sexually. But I do want to feel free to come from my own sexual needs."

At first, Matthew complained, "I wish this would all go away. It's like a bad nightmare." Then, with a sound of resolve in his voice, he said, "Okay. I understand you feel pushed. I know I can't just get my way even though I want to. Let's see if we can find a way that works for both of us."

It was finally time to brainstorm a new solution. Although not likely to be perfect, perhaps it would open the door to new sexual experiences, new approaches to being oneself in bed. They tried out a variety of ideas, each of which didn't work because they put the responsibility for the problem on the other person. Just as I was about to point this out, a light bulb went on for Julie.

"Wait a minute," she said. "I've just realized something. I know I'd like to spend more time cuddling, talking, and feeling close rather than jumping into bed to have intercourse. If that's what I want, I shouldn't ask you to make it happen. I should make it happen myself. I have to initiate our intimate times!"

At first Matthew was unsure. After the sexual disappointment in his first marriage, he doubted that Julie really meant what she said and thought she would never follow through. He also wanted to make sure he still had his own sexual freedom. He said, "I hope you can also do it my way at times—when I initiate sex."

After talking more, and with Julie reassuring him, he finally said, "Hmm, it might be interesting for you to take the lead. I'd like to know more about what you mean by 'intimate' times. I'm for it."

By the time Julie and Matthew had ended their conversation, they had decided on a range of sexual options. Most important, they had agreed that during the next week, Julie would be the one to initiate their intimate time and so lead the way. Matthew would take his turn the following week. Then they would talk about their reactions and decide what to do next.

The person who initiates sex always runs the risk of rejection. Even if two people are very attracted to each other, at that particular moment their separate bodies might be giving them separate messages. One solution, if it feels right to both people, is to take some interactive time and see what happens. Instead of a quick yes or no, the more loving answer might be "maybe—let's be close and see what happens." Of course, the final answer may still be no, but this too can be given and received with care. And fortunately, sexual desire can be satisfied personally as well as interactively.

Matthew and Julie were learning to express their individual needs, hear the other's needs, and use their capacity for double vision to hold both in mind. They came up with a course of action that, though it might not solve the problem completely, held the promise of change. They were learning to use their intention to move toward resonance.

As it turns out, the plan did work—not perfectly but well enough to break the ice. They began to play in bed again. With separate sexual voices, they took a step toward being connected in a mutually satisfying way.

Seven Things to Remember as You Search for Resonant Sex

1. Resonant intention begins with a vision of the best you can be sexually. It continues with dreaming, wishing, or intentionally planning to make the vision real.

2. Pleasure is a good in itself and a vehicle for sexual development. This should be self-evident, but many contradictory messages exist in our society: "It feels so good it must be bad." "Anything this good has to be immoral or illegal."

3. Fantasy and play, "as if" thought and behavior, are well suited to sexuality, as long as you maintain the boundary between this make-believe world and the real world.

4. Erotic freedom emerges as you focus on your own sexual thoughts and feelings, proudly. Sexual intimacy emerges as you use your double vision to know your own and your partner's body.

5. Letting go of gender prescriptions fosters the search for resonance by allowing you to know your own unique sexual self—a self that is some combination of traditionally masculine and feminine qualities.

6. If you and your partner forego the attempt at control (except through play) you'll feel safe enough to embrace your sexuality fully.

7. Resonant sex is most likely to occur in intimate time, those moments when you and another person create a rhythm together. That's the rhythm that connects and at the same time allows for individual improvisation. You might discover the peak sexual experience—when all our various clocks stand still and both people feel part of a glorious, larger whole.

Common Blocks to Sexual Resonance: A Diagnosis

An essential step toward resonance involves understanding what isn't working in your sex life right now, and why. Here are some common complaints I hear from clients—and a likely diagnosis of the underlying problem.

He: I just can't seem to turn her on.
She: He's driving me crazy. All he wants is sex, sex, sex.

The Problem: Sometimes people who can't connect sexually keep trying but only in the same old way. If a solution doesn't work, another needs to be tried. Good sex needs honest talk, play, creativity, fun. Then it's more likely that you'll find the right interactive beat.

He: I feel guilty. I keep thinking of other women—even when I'm in bed with my wife.
She: If he doesn't want to be with me, he can leave!

The Problem: When a sexual relationship is in trouble, people often think of finding someone else. Rushing toward another relationship is one approach. Another approach is to face the problem, talk about what's going wrong without blame, and if that doesn't work, seek help.

He: Why can't she just say yes to my desires, to satisfy me?
She: I'm not his slave!

The Problem: You're in a battle for power and control. It's extremely important to your sex life to find a way out of it. He might try talking openly about his sexual desires and she might try talking about her own. Perhaps, with the use of double vision, they might find a way to satisfy each other so that no one feels forced.

He: She's uptight.
She: He's disgusting.

The Problem: It's often easier to blame than to explore personal feelings about sex. Focus in on the reasons for your own attitudes. Also, listen without judgment to your partner, even if you feel unable to meet his or her needs. It's important to grasp the one-of-a-kind quality of your union. Your idiosyncrasies make it all the more interesting.

She: I'm not much to look at. I can't blame him if he wants someone else.
He: If I can't satisfy her, I'm not much of a lover.

The Problem: Ultimately, it isn't looks or technique that leads to good sex. It's your capacity to feel your erotic desire, to sense your partner's desire, and to be open to exploring it all.

She: Oh, well. Sex isn't everything.
He: How can I marry her? Sexually, she just isn't my type.

The Problem: Sex is central to our lives. Both partners need to feel "right" with each other, but not perfect—that's not likely for human beings. Most important, each partner needs to commit to the development of their sexual union.

She: He never asks me to make love anymore, so I try to make it happen.
He: I'm uncomfortable when she's the aggressor.

The Problem: You're sexual relationship is probably stuck in a prescription that says men should initiate and women should submit. Ultimately, this doesn't work. Learn who you are as a sexual person and how that fits with, and differs from, prescribed role behavior.

CHAPTER 11

The Money Tool

... the cost of things is the amount of what I call
life which is required to be exchanged for it,
immediately or in the long run.
—Henry David Thoreau, *Walden*

Carlene sat stiffly in her chair, a pair of Laura Biagiotti sunglasses hiding her eyes, and a Hermes scarf cleverly tied around her head to conceal her bandages. Her smile was determined, but her jaw was tight with discomfort. Two days ago she had cosmetic surgery—this time a face-lift.

For a moment I wasn't sure how to connect with the woman inside all these wrappings, but then she spoke, "The surgeon was expensive. Still, he's the best, and what can you expect? But John is complaining about the money, just as he always does. This morning he even brought up the car. I want to trade it—I hate the way it handles—but he thinks it's crazy to trade a car that's less than a year old."

Money, and the things that money buys, were the ground upon which John and Carlene were fighting a raging and vicious

marital battle. Carlene's most recent spending spree included re-
decorating two rooms in the house, planning another trip to Eu-
rope, and her latest whim to trade her six-month-old Lexus for a
new car.

As we discussed the meaning of all of this spending, it struck
me that Carlene had begun this therapy hour talking about the
fight she was having with her husband over money. Why, I won-
dered, wasn't she talking about her body, the operation, the discomfort she was still experiencing?

When I asked her how she was feeling, she almost dismissed my
concern, but finally said, "I was scared before the operation. You
know, I'm terribly frightened of hospitals and surgery."

She then quickly shifted the conversation back to her complaints about John. "He ignored the whole thing. He didn't even
come to the hospital. How could he be such a bastard?"

I tried one more time. "Does it hurt?" I asked, nodding toward
her bandages.

She allowed herself only these words: "I'm uncomfortable. My
skin feels tight; it's very tender to the touch. I couldn't sleep last
night at all."

Before I could reply, she went back to her obsession with getting a new car and John's attempt to deny her money when what
he makes easily covers what she spends.

Carlene rarely talked about how she felt inside, or her physical
well-being, because she learned early in life that it did no good—
no one would listen. Her anger and her sadness came out anyway,
and when that happened, she bought things. But no matter how
much she bought, something was always missing. Even so, she
continued to believe that the next purchase would make her
happy. It did, for a few brief moments. Then her anger and sadness would return.

Carlene didn't understand that her unhappiness wasn't about
things but about her inability to give and receive love. John had a
similar problem.

Relationships like this follow a predictable pattern: Feeling deprived of love, John blamed Carlene, and so he only begrudgingly gave her his money, his substitute for love. Because money can't really take the place of love, Carlene also felt deprived. So she blamed him and angrily threw his money away. Then John felt even more deprived of love.

In a circular fashion, blame and deprivation run through each person, tying them together in a vicious embrace. As I watched Carlene stride out of my office that day, I couldn't help but think how ironic it was that she and John were the envy of so many of their friends.

For many couples, continued conflict over money forms a kind of glue that keeps them connected—and also disguises a host of more vulnerable feelings, such as fear, sadness, guilt, even love. Are battles over money a frequent event in your relationship? Do you feel that your partner spends too much? Do you feel he or she doesn't understand how to handle finances? That he or she is selfish when it comes to money?

Have you ever hidden money from your partner? Has the struggle to earn enough begun to consume too much of your and/or your partner's energy? Have you ever thought that your problems would disappear if you just had more money?

If you answered yes to any of these statements, you're not alone. Battles like these are prevalent in many relationships, and that's why it's important to find more creative ways of dealing with money.

What if you could learn to use money so that it nourishes you both individually and as a couple? What if you could resolve your conflicts about money so that neither of you came out feeling like a loser? Best of all, what if you could use your money to play and have fun, to enhance your love and fuel your passion?

This is precisely what happens when couples use money to search for resonance. Resonant couples face the same pressures and challenges most of us do. Some struggle to make enough to meet their monthly bills. In many cases, each partner has a markedly different idea about how money should be spent. Yet they are able to create a way of managing money that leads to resonance. What can these people teach the rest of us?

Trouble and Success with Money

The couples you'll meet in the following pages struggled over money, sometimes to the point where it almost cost them their relationships. Change came as a result of very important and necessary decisions: They paid serious attention to their conflict over money and were intent on exploring their underlying emotional and developmental needs. They respected the fact that they each had individual financial needs as well as shared financial needs. Finally, they identified individual as well as shared financial goals and created a shared process for achieving them.

Most important, what stands out in their stories is that they grasped the truth that money is a tool. It can destroy any possibility of resonance, or it can help bring a unique vision of love to life.

■ David and Gail: All Work and No Play

A wrong turn on a suburban street was the start of Gail's inspiration for a business of her own. She turned her car around in a driveway, and her eyes fell on a for sale sign, almost hidden by overgrown shrubbery. The square, old, two-story house was weatherbeaten, but ideas for remodeling it immediately ran through her mind. "What a charming place for an antique store," she mused, "and I bet I could buy it with the money I inherited after Dad's death." On impulse she met with the real estate agent that same afternoon. She quit her part-time job selling jewelry and, a month later, started her own business. The antique store thrived, but

Gail's marriage hit real trouble. By the time she got the kids to school, worked a full day at her store, picked the kids up from their lessons, ate dinner, and then settled down to tally the day's receipts, she had little energy left for David, her husband.

When David's company cut 20 percent of its staff to battle the recession, he feared his position could be next and began to work longer hours than he ever had, hoping to increase his value to the company. Exhausted and frustrated, he started to explode at Gail. He complained that she never paid attention to him anymore and accused her of being obsessed with her store.

Gail admitted to thinking, "For the first time in my adult life, I can support myself. Why do I need him or this aggravation? I shouldn't have to answer to anyone for my time or my financial decisions. If David isn't going to help me, the least he can do is get out of my way while I help myself."

The question underneath David's anger and Gail's exhaustion haunts many couples today: What should come first, love or money? Do we get married even though he doesn't have a good job? Do I move a thousand miles because she got a promotion? Do I stay home now that there's a second child?

If our primary goal is to make money, we talk of interest rates, money market funds, job strategies, and raises and pensions, and the decisions we make shape the rest of our lives. If we're looking for resonance, we talk about life goals for ourselves and our relationships, about trust, play, and intimacy, and these conversations shape the way we make and manage money.

In search of resonance, we ask questions like: How will money be used in the service of each person? How can money be used to further the experience of union, of intimacy? What beliefs do we have about money, and where do those beliefs come from? Do they work for us? Or, are we simply following the lead of others?

Gail and David were collapsing under the strain of their beliefs about money—their financial system was undermining their union. The cart was leading the horse, and they didn't even know it.

In my experience, some beliefs about money are life-restricting for individuals and families. Other beliefs are life-enhancing and encourage relationships in which resonance becomes possible. Consider the following beliefs:

Life-restricting: Money is in and of itself a good thing and worth pursing as a goal in its own right.

Life-enhancing: Money isn't good or bad. It's nothing more or less than a very powerful tool. When you're clear about your larger life goals, you can intentionally use the money tool to achieve them.

Life-restricting: The more money you make, the better your life will be.

Life-enhancing: More doesn't always mean better. Only one hammer can be used at a time, and if it isn't used correctly, it can do damage. Using money consciously to enhance the quality of your inner life and your relationship is a step toward resonance.

Life-restricting: The natural by-product of financial success is control over people, and that's a good thing to have.

Life-enhancing: Money can offer such control, but the people who feel controlled are likely to become angry and resentful. This can lead to relationships that are financial tyrannies. You can also use money to share power, thereby enhancing your relationships.

Life-restricting: Money can make you secure.

Life-enhancing: Ultimately, living is not a secure experience. Money can only bring material security provided the rest of the world remains stable, the economic system continues to function adequately, and one's investments retain their value. This has little do with the sense of safety you can find in loving relationships.

Life-restricting: Never use your principal ... Always borrow as much as you can ... Never buy on credit ... Save 10 percent of each paycheck . . . Don't spend more than a third of your paycheck on rent . . . Don't improve your house beyond its market value . . . Always act to shelter your income from taxes . . . and so on.

Life-enhancing: Such out-of-context rules are used by many people, especially trust officers, accountants, or financial investment advisers. They usually work to make money grow, not to enhance the quality of your personal life. While it's important to get advice, financial rules need to be shaped and applied personally, so they further the larger goals of life. Decision making is, and must remain, a personal act.

Gail and David explored their beliefs about money and learned how those beliefs restricted their lives. It was an eye-opener. If their money was a tool, a means to an end, what were their larger goals?

The answers to this question triggered several changes. Most important, David and Gail became an economic partnership with the commitment to help each other. David then decided to reduce his time at work. Making himself a slave to a job he disliked put money in the bank but at too high a cost. He and Gail had many lengthy conversations about the steps they would take if he did lose his job. Gail stopped opening her shop on Sundays and is working, in therapy, to learn to delegate tasks to other people rather than doing everything herself.

She said recently, "I guess I thought that if I was successful in business, I'd be happy. I just assumed my relationship would somehow stand the strain."

Now David and Gail regularly set aside time for themselves, intentionally shifting away from the hectic pace of work into the intimate time that nourishes their relationship.

With or without intention, money continually shapes our lives. We do best when we consciously think about larger life goals and then use money to reach those goals—knowing that as any tool is used, the product itself alters in shape.

What kind of work, family, and spiritual life do we want at age twenty-five, and how will it change at forty-five, or sixty-five? What will happen if we try the very best we can to create a successful financial life, and for one reason or another—loss of a job, illness, or aging—we meet with failure? What will we be left with? Perhaps less money. But if the experience of building an economic life is cooperative, compassionate, and competent, the effort itself will be a success—and something of the highest value will remain.

▪ Matt and Sandra: The Saver and the Spendthrift

From the look of the three cars in their garage, one would never expect that Sandra and Matt were a couple who had to fight about spending money for their son's birthday party.

"Pony rides? A magician? Are you out of your mind?" Matt said, listening to her plan. "Why do you always go overboard? I work too hard for my money to have you throw it away on parties."

"You're cheap with your own son," she retorted hotly. "And I'm getting sick of the way you treat me like a child, like I don't have a brain in my head."

The argument that followed was so upsetting they had to separate for a while; Sandra went to pick up their son at a friend's house, and Matt escaped to his office.

Five years ago, when their baby was born, Sandra had willingly given up her career as a surgical nurse. At the time she had Matt's full approval. Then came recurring flare-ups over money. Soon they were arguing over every single purchase.

"It isn't that we can't afford these things," Sandra complained bitterly. "The more he makes, the more he worries. I never dreamed that at age thirty-five I would have to answer to an angry man whenever I needed cash to run the house."

Matt's story was different. Like many entrepreneurs, he reinvests his profits so that his business can continue to grow. "I might look rich on paper," he said, "but my cash flow is always tight."

Matt also had fears that he didn't share with his wife. He had an inner voice that foretold failure. He believed that no matter how hard he worked, his business would fail. With his self-esteem so tightly tied to his earnings, he was sure that if he had no money, Sandra would have no use for him.

In therapy, he became aware that his fear of failure and loss were rooted in his early life and that making good money helped him manage those fears. Controlling his wife's spending was another way to manage his fears—he felt safe if she didn't spend. And he hoped that as long as Sandra needed his money, she would need him.

Matt, with Sandra's cooperation, had created a family economy that was designed to allay his fear of failure and loss. It worked: His dollars grew and his wife was beholden. But by the time I met them, neither partner felt any passion for the other, only a mistrust mixed with an active contempt.

I call this kind of marital economy a financial tyranny. The tyrant assumes control while the subject feels powerless. However, when it comes to couple relationships, the roles also reverse: The tyrant can feel controlled by the subject, who uses covert power to fight back by being irresponsible about money. If winning is important enough, the battle can become exceedingly hostile.

Sandra felt powerless because her very wallet was being controlled. But Matt also felt powerless. Since he didn't do any of the buying, he had very little real control over how money was being spent. In their different ways, both people felt controlled by the other.

How does a couple escape from a financial tyranny? They can do what many couples do—both can work and keep their money separate. That works for many people. Alternatively, they can create a mutually respectful financial union; joining together while respecting their individual rights and desires. That's a resonant design.

Through therapy, Sandra and Matt realized that their financial problem was an expression of more personal issues. Sandra realized how readily she accepted the powerless role. Matt realized control was how he managed his fear of failure and loss.

"I gave up even thinking about how much money we had or where it came from," Sandra said. "All I cared about was having enough to spend. Now I see that I gave away my own power. I became a victim."

"I lived in fear that when I came home one night you wouldn't be there," Matt told her. "All I could think to do about it was to give you very little money. I was making my fear come true."

As Sandra and Matt talked about these issues, they began their search for resonance. Understanding that they both wanted to feel appreciated and valued, they tackled the problem at hand from a new perspective.

"What kind of birthday party do you want Dale to have?" Sandra asked her husband, open for the first time to really listening.

"Of course I want him to have pony rides and everything else," Matt said. "He's my son! But will he grow up thinking he's got it easy, that I can deliver colleges and cars and everything he wants?"

There is often a moment like this when couples sense the idea of resonance. Here was a goal they both shared—the passing on of certain values to their son. Suddenly they saw money as a tool that could be used to help achieve it. They listened to each other's needs, considered their total income and the financial demands they faced, and then found a way to allocate their money for each person's needs and for the needs of the union.

Do you sense you're involved in a financial tyranny? If you're in the "tyrant" role, do you realize how little real power you have, and how much anger and resentment your role generates? Are your battles over money your way of expressing anger over something else entirely? What fears does your attempt at control soothe?

If you're in the "subject" role, do you know you have given away your power? Do you have hidden fears about too much autonomy? When we hold money over other people's heads like a whip, and use it to control them or to force their love, we can only have a shaky kind of financial tyranny. When financial goals are developed with awareness of underlying fears, and with respect for each person and respect for the union, we set the stage for resonance.

▪ Kerry and Brooke: Will You Still Love Me When You No Longer Need Me?

When they were still engaged, Kerry, the owner of a small public relations firm, encouraged Brooke to leave teaching and join his firm. He taught her how to pitch stories to the news media, how to make presentations to corporations, and how to woo clients away from other agencies. Brooke was an eager and gifted student.

When a client asked Kerry to design a direct mail advertising program to promote a new restaurant, Kerry handed the project over to Brooke. The program she designed won an award as well as hundreds of new customers for the client. So much direct mail business followed in the next few years that Kerry and Brooke opened Direct to You, an offshoot company focused specifically on direct mail advertising, with Brooke at the helm.

Kerry managed the finances of the new company as well as the PR firm, which was okay with Brooke in the beginning. But as her company became more successful, Kerry became tighter with money and more critical of her.

"To this day, he's critical of the salaries I pay," Brooke complained. "He tells me when I should raise my rates and to check with him before I buy any new equipment for the business. After all I've done for this company, in his eyes I'm still his student."

One night when Brooke was alone at the office, she opened the computer program that tracked money in both her and her husband's firms. She was shocked to find that Direct to You was earning more money than her husband's firm, and it had been for some time.

When Brooke and Kerry first came to see me, they argued so vehemently for the first fifteen minutes that I said, "This is going nowhere," and asked one of them to sit in the waiting room while I spoke with the other.

Kerry's side was simple. He said, "Brooke isn't going to tell me what to do. She can't even keep her books straight; she's terrible with numbers. She wouldn't even have this company if it wasn't for me. I gave her the first account, taught her everything I know, and then she has the nerve to talk before the Chamber of Commerce as if the business is all hers! She even wants to legally own a part of the business, putting it in her own name in trust for her parents. They wouldn't give us the time of day when we married. If they think I'm ever going to support them, they'll be waiting a long time."

After this flash of anger, Kerry met my eyes and shook his head slowly. "I'm afraid that Brooke is pushing me out of the business. She's got so much talent. It took me by surprise at first; she has writing skills I'll never have. I used to love helping her. Now I hate talking business with her. When people don't need you, they have no time for you. They don't listen, even when you're right."

Brooke felt manipulated and misused. For years the man she lived with was lying to her about the success of her business, depriving her of good feelings that come with knowing you're a winner. In private, she told me she wanted to own the business by herself.

There's a basic choice to be made in family life. Either we ask others to give to us out of love, and we do the same for them, or we try to force them to satisfy our needs. Forcing love doesn't work. In fact, it's destructive. But that doesn't stop people from trying. In the ensuing battle, everyone becomes too well-defended to imagine asking for what they need.

In all of their years of working together, Kerry never talked with his wife about his fear of losing the role of mentor or teacher and founder of the business. Nor did he ask for help. Instead, he tried to force Brooke to continue to accept his authority.

Similarly, Brooke never talked directly about her desire for more autonomy. She flattered and submitted to Kerry on the outside, and when she thought he wasn't looking, she tried to tear away from him.

There's always hope when people talk as honestly as these two did that day in my office. Honest self-reflection can diminish hostility and allow a couple to focus inside themselves to understand their emotional as well as their material desires. If that goes well, they might even be able to use their double vision to know the other without losing a sense of themselves.

Over the next few months Kerry and Brooke did just that, developing life-enhancing purposes for their money as well. Ultimately, they reorganized their business so that Brooke felt more autonomy and Kerry still felt somewhat needed.

Relationships have developmental needs, just like individuals do. It's hard, and fraught with a sense of risk, for two people who once let one person lead and the other follow to begin to be equally present in the relationship. Then, decisions about money become more complex. Where before one decided and the other complained, now both must ask of themselves and of each other, "What is best for me? What is best for you? What is best for us?" They must be willing to engage in a loving and inevitable struggle over issues of power that play themselves out in their joint economy. And they must be willing to give up that false but seductive sense of security that comes from having power over another.

Letting go and feeling safe can lead a couple to be themselves together.

▪ *Benjamin and Sheila: I'm Not Going To Support
Another Man's Children!*

Sheila and Benjamin, married for about a year, each had children from their previous marriages. Although Benjamin had three
children, only his sixteen-year-old daughter lived with them. The
other two attended college on the West Coast. All of Sheila's children, two young sons and a fourteen-year-old daughter, Aimee,
lived with them.

As an investment broker, Benjamin made a salary well into six
figures. All of his children drove the new cars, which he bought
them for their birthdays, and he took them away on expensive vacations several times a year.

It was different for Sheila. Her ex-husband only grudgingly
provided child support. She had to fight for every small check.

Benjamin was willing to support the family's lifestyle. He paid
their sizable mortgage and other ongoing household expenses.
"But I'm not going to support his kids," he once said, furious over
another late child-support check.

Sheila used her salary and the child-support checks to pay for
all the expenses associated with her children, as well as smaller
items like food and cleaning expenses. Sheila, who hated to see
her children without the things their friends had, found little left
from her salary for herself.

When Aimee, Sheila's fourteen-year-old daughter, was caught
tearing the tags off a designer dress and attempting to wear it out
of the store, both parents were shocked.

"She doesn't need more clothes," Benjamin said, frustrated.
"She takes up more closet space than anyone else in the family.
She wastes all of her money on junk when she should be saving
for college. Trouble is, Sheila lets her get away with it."

To me, Aimee's shoplifting made perfect sense. Because they
started out with markedly different incomes, Sheila and Benjamin
had created a two-class system inside their own home—the haves

and the have-nots. Aimee responded to the inequality by trying to tip the scales in her direction.

This couple had set up two separate financial systems. They had an exchange relationship that kept "her" family and "his" family apart. It protected Benjamin from having to support Aimee's children and soothed his fear that their biological father was taking advantage of him. But it kept the adults watching the numbers, and it made some children winners and others losers.

"Splitting it down the middle" is often an attempt at fairness, but it can hide the reality that one person usually earns more than the other. It's also an attempt at safety: Chances are one person is worrying that the other will gain the advantage, taking more than he or she gives. And if anything should go wrong, they both know they will leave with what is theirs.

A couple may have good reasons for this kind of exchange economy. It may seem the safer route. But to experience resonance, people do both—they use money to satisfy individual needs and the needs of their union. A man like Benjamin needs to respect his desire not to support another man's children, but he also needs a union that feels supportive of both partners.

Ultimately, Sheila and Benjamin decided to create a resonant economy. The result wasn't perfect, but it was better than anything they had tried before: They created a pool of income (underwritten more by him than by her) to support everyone. With that money they funded a checking account for his expenses, one for hers, and one that paid for all family expenses, including a clothing allowance for each of the children. Benjamin used other money to buy special gifts for his children. While they still got more than Sheila's children did, the basic support was the same for everyone.

Benjamin did indeed contribute to the support of another man's children, but less than he had originally feared. Most important, he developed a financial union that worked better for him and Sheila and their family.

Money can satisfy separate needs and nourish a union. The following couple offer another, more fully satisfying example.

▪ *Cathy and Donald: You're Just Like Your Mother!*

Cathy grew up in a family that used money as a weapon. Her mother lived by the rule "a penny saved is a penny earned," while her father could often be heard saying, "What's money for, except to spend?" As a youngster, Cathy felt her mother made more sense.

Cathy, now a programmer for a large pharmaceutical company, is married to Donald, who does the same work and makes about the same money. But he's much freer with money than she is. For instance, Cathy thought they should be saving for the time when they will have children. Donald didn't agree. "If we need more money, I'll make it," he told her, with a confidence in the future Cathy couldn't share if her life depended on it.

Donald's mother and father were supreme consumers, people who confused money with love. Donald patterned his behavior after them. He still has no problem knocking on his father's door when things are tight. He couldn't understand why Cathy found this humiliating.

"My parents can afford to help out," he said. "They bail my sister and brother out every other week."

If you want a resonant economy, it's important to make your financial system an expression of your own union. That involves drawing a boundary that allows you to reconsider your parent's, friend's, neighbor's, or co-worker's approach to money. Cathy and Donald did this. They traced their money behavior back to their parents, reconsidered it in the light of their current needs, and went on to develop an approach of their own.

That meant focusing on their individual financial needs, talking about their shared needs, and using money to satisfy all this. The effort itself enhanced their union.

Not too long ago, Donald gave a dinner party for some of his colleagues. He wanted to serve lobster, and Cathy argued for the less expensive roast chicken. This time, they laughed when they realized that without thinking they were polarizing just like Cathy's parents did.

Donald said, "We talked about what the dinner meant to each of us, trying to find a way to agree. Finally, we compromised on a lamb and vegetable dish and a chocolate mousse—my favorite dessert. We each did some of the buying and some of the cooking, and we both entertained the group."

In the end, that dinner became an expression of Cathy and Donald, not of either of their families or some rendition of the correct rules of etiquette. Cathy and Donald used their money as a shared tool.

Creating a Resonant Economy

The questions that haunt us about money and the fights we have become easier to understand, if not resolve, when larger human goals—and the process of moving toward those goals—are kept in mind. If we want experiences of quality and relationships of resonance, we will make use of all the tools we have at hand, including money. And while creating a resonant economy is not always easy, the underlying principles are as follows.

Learn from your conflicts over money.

Consider your typical financial disagreement: Do you fight about who makes the money? How it's allocated? Who spends it? Use your double vision to understand each other, and appreciate the function money plays in the attempt to solve each person's life issues. Then plan for the likelihood of other financial conflicts, so that you will be ready to react creatively.

After Matthew and Dorothy's last spending spree, resulting in an overdrawn checking account, they felt guilty and angry at themselves for being so irresponsible. It took several days and lots of talk to get over it. They couldn't help but recognize that ignoring limits was a pattern in their lives—not only when they bought things but when they partied too hard. They decided the state of their finances was too important for them to keep going from crisis to crisis. They did their budget, as they had in the past, but this time they didn't tuck it away in a drawer—they hung it on their refrigerator. Now it wouldn't be so easy to ignore.

Develop financial goals with respect for each other and the union.

Take responsibility for exploring the relationship between money and your own developmental needs. Then create a set of wishes, dreams, and in some cases, actual goals for yourself. Ask your partner to do the same. With clarity about each person's needs and about the shared needs of the union, consider your total income and the financial demands you face. Allocate dollars for each person's needs and for the needs of the union.

Develop a structure for handling money.

Merged couples tend to underfund the "I" and exchange couples underfund the "we." When money is a tool that's used to foster resonance, each "I" as well as the "we" are funded—none of the three are slighted.

There are many financial strategies that can help. For instance, you might minimize the difference in income between you and your partner by creating a pool of income money for all the expenses. One person might contribute more to the pool than the other, but the union and the money belongs to both of them. Three checking accounts can be funded out of that pool, one for each person and one for the household—with enough dollars in each to cover expenses. If there's any money left, it can go into a savings account and be used for future dreams, clearly identified as his, hers, and theirs.

Whatever financial vehicles are used, if money is to be a tool to serve a resonant relationship, each person needs a separate voice and a desire to live within the larger whole called the union. Resonant intention in the form of wishing, dreaming, and careful planning is also part of the process.

Allocate money for play.

It's all too easy for busy adults to forget that play is nourishing—without it, the children we still are feel deprived. Money can be the tool that sets the stage for play. If you think of your play time, what comes to mind? A day at the beach? A trip to the Caribbean? Time off? Dinner at a good restaurant with friends? Whichever, it's likely to be something you do for yourself or some activity that heightens the pleasure of being together. It's likely to be something that has little purpose except the enjoyment that occurs when you access the world through your five senses.

Make play a part of your budget. And even when the call of work is loudest, remember to listen to the inner voice that says, "I also need to have fun."

CHAPTER 12

On the Road to Resonance

Exercises for You and Your Partner

The exercises in this chapter can help you stretch toward resonance in your relationship. If possible, do each exercise with your partner, and don't deny yourself the time and privacy you need, even if it means leaving the house and getting a sitter. The exercises require your complete attention—and a child in need or the ringing of a telephone can break the spell.

Read through each exercise before you begin, and then go back to the beginning and do them step by step. Keep separate journals to record your responses as they occur. Even though some exercises may seem more appealing to you than others, you'll benefit most if you work through them all in order.

If you escalate into hostility or extreme discomfort during any of these exercises, stop. Take some time out, and then get together to read the chapter that considers the issue causing trouble. If you're really stuck, skip that exercise and return to it later. Sometimes it's better to go around a problem rather than pushing your way through it.

Never forget to congratulate each other on your search for resonance despite the inevitable crises along the way. Two excellent books that persuasively argue the power of positive thinking are Shelly Taylor's *Positive Illusions* and George Valliant's *Adaption to Life*. Seeing the half-full glass goes a long way toward managing the half-empty aspects of human life.

Exercise One: Finding Resonance

Part I. Setting the Ground Rules

Resonance is more likely to occur when we feel safe. For this reason, it's important to learn how to draw mental boundaries around yourself, to keep some people out and let others in.

In the following set of experiences, you will at times draw that imaginary line around yourself and at other times around you and your partner. These boundaries come with a special "bill of rights." Anyone inside has the right to be treated as a "thou"—an extraordinary person, a vital spirit, one who is vulnerable and needs protection. To establish such boundaries, read the following statement, and both sign your names.

> "I hold these experiences to be special. I will never use anything that happens during one of them to threaten or demean my partner. I will never share anything that takes place between us with anyone else unless my partner gives permission."
>
> Signatures:
>
> _____
>
> _____

Part II. Inner Resonance

During this part of the exercise, you'll explore your personal experiences of resonance, which will help you with interactive resonance. Work through the following exercise alone, jotting down notes in your journal. When you both finish, share your results.

Recall a peak personal experience. Perhaps it was playing tennis, and the ball always seemed to fall in just the right spot. Perhaps you won a poker game, or you placed first in a race. Maybe it was a moment when you felt awed by your child's smile or witnessed a magnificent sunset.

Close your eyes and picture the place where it occurred. Make the memory come alive. If it was inside, see the room—the ceiling, the floor, the furniture. If it was outside, see the sky and the landscape, feel the weather. What is your felt sense of the memory? Did your chest feel like bursting? Did your head feel giddy? Was there a feeling of fullness? Do you feel it now?

Listen to what your inner voice is saying. Pay attention to your thoughts. Can you hear a sound like ahhhh, or a word like amazing? Don't worry if what you hear or think sounds childlike.

When you are finished imagining the moment, take as long as you need to write about the experience and any feelings you have about it.

Share your results with your partner.

Part III. Interactive Resonance

It's likely that you have also had such peak experiences of resonance with your partner. Remembering them is important because they can serve as guideposts—examples of what is possible in the future.

Again, by yourself, recall a special moment in your relationship. Perhaps it was a time of great significance—the moment when you first met, when you knew you were in love, or when you had your first child. Perhaps it was a small moment, a walk in the park or on the beach. If you have trouble finding a memory, look through a photograph album.

Reminisce by yourself for a few moments. Where did it happen? What was the time of day? What were you doing? See if you can remember the felt sense of the experience. Perhaps your breath came faster or you had a moment of super-clear vision. Listen to what your inner voice has to say. Perhaps you thought you were one of the luckiest couples in the world.

Record your thoughts.

As you tell each other your memories, paint the physical picture in detail, recalling where the resonant experience took place, the time of day, and what you were doing.

Most important, don't expect that your partner will have the same memory or the same felt sense. Maybe she didn't feel the same rush of excitement the first time you met. Perhaps he doesn't remember that moonlit night five years ago; instead, he remembers a moment on the interstate, with the two of you alone on the long open road. One memory isn't better than the other. Resonant loving includes valuing our separateness as well as our connection.

Part IV. Envisioning the Future

By recalling peak experiences of resonance, you have made it more likely that you will have them in the future.

Together, imagine a peak experience of resonance in the future. Envision what the setting might be, the time, the activity that might trigger the experience. Perhaps the two of you would feel most in tune dancing or lying on a smooth, white beach. Why are these conditions perfect? How likely is it that you can make them happen?

Now celebrate. Having completed the first exercise, take a moment to affirm your search for resonance. A quiet word of thanks might be all that's called for. It's an affirmation of you, your partner, and your union. Set a time for the next exercise.

Exercise Two: Changing Patterns That Interfere with Resonance

Part I. Taking a Closer Look at the Balance Between Independence and Closeness

This exercise explores an important and very common relationship pattern—the pull between independence and closeness. Partners tend to stretch in opposite directions, especially when they are stressed. Find out how that happens in your relationship.

To begin, find a private place where others can't hear you.

Together, select one of the following independence/closeness conflicts. Or, invent one of your own, but make sure the situation doesn't seem very important in your relationship. Practicing is easier when the content isn't highly charged.

One of you wants to go away for a vacation alone and the other wants to go together.

One of you spends impulsively and the other wants to plan expenditures jointly.

One of you wants to decorate the living room alone and the other wants to do it together.

You should each choose the role that feels most familiar to you. Now, take turns expressing your points of view. Stop when you both recognize that the conflict is essentially about one person's need for independence and the other's need for closeness.

Silently focus inside on your felt sense of the role. Perhaps you're the one who can't breathe comfortably unless you're free to do your own thing. Maybe you're the one who can't relax until you're close enough to feel safe.

Pay attention to your inner voice. Remember, if you tend to stretch toward personal freedom, you're likely to worry about being held back or even engulfed. And if you tend to stretch toward closeness, you're likely to worry about being alone or abandoned. Write about what you feel.

Share what you each learn about yourselves. Your goal is to listen without judgment and to empathize.

Now, take the opposite role. Repeat the previous three steps, only this time from the other person's point of view. For example, if you tend to focus on your independence, shift roles so that you focus on closeness. While it's difficult to make a shift like this, doing it will help you understand your partner's feelings, which is a step toward the double vision necessary to find mutual solutions to real-life conflicts.

First write in your journal and then talk about what you have learned. Can you recognize both sides of the polarity inside yourself?

Part II. Discovering Family Roots

Because most interpersonal patterns are learned early in life, you can probably trace your role in the independence/closeness polarity back to childhood. Chances are, your parents enacted a rendition of this pattern in their relationship, and you reacted to it when you were a child.

Working alone, focus on the scene you enacted in the first part of this exercise, once again assuming your preferred role. Let your mind wander back in time until you remember an early family experience that made you feel either overwhelmed and engulfed or alone and abandoned.

Did you feel abandoned, rejected, or unloved the first time you were left at school or camp? The moment you learned that your parents were separating? When a parent was too busy to listen to you or help with your homework?

Did you feel engulfed or possessed when your father yelled at you or hit you? When your mother demanded you tell her what you did with a friend? When a parent checked your homework to make it perfect?

Once you settle on a memory, close your eyes and recall it in more detail. Where did it take place? What did the room look like? Can you see the faces of those who were present? Look for a felt sense of the experience and listen to your inner voice. Record what you have learned in your journal.

Take turns sharing your memories with each other. Once again, avoid any personal or judgmental statements as you listen. By empathizing with each other's feelings, you create a relationship in which the pain of the past can be healed. When you give each other the experience of feeling close without feeling possessed, and of feeling separate without feeling alone, you create a holistic, both/and experience—both personal freedom and closeness—and that's essential to resonance.

Take a moment to enjoy the work you're doing together. Set a time for the next exercise.

Exercise Three: Developing Resonant Power

Part I. Heightening Your Power to Give and Receive Nurturing

As a couple, you each are important in each other's lives, and this gives you tremendous power to influence each other. In this exercise, you will both experience that power, giving it and receiving it.

Place yourselves on a couch so that one person lies down and places his or her head in the lap of the other person. The person sitting up is in the more powerful, adult position. That person's task is to nurture the other without expressing his or her own thoughts. The person lying down is in the more vulnerable position. That person's task is to let him or herself be nurtured.

As the person lying down, close your eyes and silently feel yourself being nurtured by the other. Get in touch with your felt sense of the experience. Do you feel like jumping up? Is it hard to get comfortable? What does your inner voice have to say? Do you fear being too close or engulfed? Do you fear rejection? Do you feel loved? As your felt sense becomes clear, spend about fifteen minutes describing it to the other while being held in his or her lap.

Then, if you are the person sitting up, talk about your experience being in the more powerful, nurturant position. Do you feel responsible for the other person's well-being? Do you feel good, or do you feel like it's more than you can manage?

Reverse positions. Repeat the experience taking opposite roles. Then record what you have learned in your journals.

Part II. Learning to Lead and to Follow

One aspect of power is the capacity to take charge, to get what we need. But the capacity to follow is also an aspect of power, the ability to respond to another's needs. Many of us are fearful either of taking charge or of following. We don't feel safe enough and so we inhibit one or both kinds of power. This is a chance to experience both in a positive way.

This exercise depends on trust. So it's important to remember the promise you made to each other at the beginning: "I hold these experiences to be special. I will never use anything that happens during one of them to threaten or demean my partner."

Choose who will take the role of the leader and who the follower, knowing you will reverse these roles later on. Though this is play, treat it as if it were real life.

For the next thirty minutes, the person taking the role of leader will decide what the other will do. If you're in the leader's role, this is a chance to shape your partner's behavior and get your own needs met. Ask your partner to wash the dishes, iron your clothes, give you a back rub, or make you lunch. The person in the role of follower should be open to direction, forgoing any resistance unless the other's behavior is threatening or demeaning. "Please give me a back rub" feels more loving than "If you don't give me a back rub, you can forget about going out to dinner tonight."

When the thirty minutes are over, write about what you have learned. If you were the leader, did you feel strong, or did you feel confused or frightened? If you were the follower, did you feel inert, resistant, or could you yield? Describe your felt sense.

Listen to your inner voice. If you were the leader, could you hear yourself say, "I don't know what else to ask for," or "Finally, a chance to get what I want!" If you were the follower, could you hear yourself say, "No way am I going to obey," or "Finally, someone else is taking responsibility." What did your inner voice have to say? Write about what you have learned.

Switch roles and repeat the exercise.

When you are finished, gently compliment each other and talk about what you have learned. You have now experimented with two modes of power—the power to nurture and be nurtured and the power to lead and to follow. Experimenting as you have done in this exercise gives you an opportunity to understand how you might, without awareness, be resisting or abusing one or both of these modes of power, and so be contributing to the creation of an unsafe environment.

Exercise Four: Practicing Resonant Conflict

Part I. Developing Your Own Voice

Often we think that the irritations of everyday life aren't worth arguing about, but that's what most arguments are about. These conflicts are natural and unavoidable. In this exercise, you'll concentrate on how to express your anger and avoid hostility when you argue.

Working together, identify a conflict you have sharing something you both need. Does your partner spend hours in the bathroom in a way you feel is inconsiderate? Use the car without refilling the gas tank? Have long telephone conversations that interfere with calls you have to make? Choose a conflict that doesn't generate strong emotion. That will make it easier to learn conflict management skills.

Working separately, write about the problem. Let yourself be hostile but keep your thoughts on paper. In this way you can both act as if you were in a hostile fight when you really aren't. Use threats, labeling, blaming, abusive language, and sarcasm. Don't hold back!

When you feel satisfied that you have both fully expressed your hostility, tear the pages from your journal, put them in an ashtray, and burn them. By no means show them to each other. In this way you both know your own capacity for hostility—for directing your anger *at* someone you assume is totally at fault.

Now write an "I feel/I fear" statement about the conflict—an expression of the emotions behind your anger. Any of the following might approach what's happening inside:

> I feel my chest tighten when I don't have enough time to use the bathroom in the morning, and I fear you don't really care about me.
>
> I feel irritable when you talk on the telephone for a long time, and I fear that I won't get to make my calls.
>
> I feel my blood pressure rising when there isn't enough gas in the car, and I fear that I will always be taking care of you.

Facing the fears associated with conflict is no easy matter, but if you can, you're more likely to develop a separate voice—the capacity to be aware of, and stay focused on, your own perceptions. Having a separate voice is not the only skill needed to manage conflict well, however. You also need double vision.

Part II. Using Your Double Vision

In the search for resonance, it's important to hold both your own and the other person's perceptions in mind. Only then can you experience the "mutuality" that heals.

First, one of you can begin with your I feel/I fear statement.

Ask your partner to paraphrase what you've said, making clear his or her understanding of your point of view. Modify those comments until you feel understood.

Now switch and repeat the exercise.

Part III. Brainstorming a New Synthesis

Managing conflict well involves holding your own and your partner's feelings and fears in mind and looking for a resolution that answers both your needs. Recall that the perfect both/and synthesis is sometimes hard to find; often it's only a satisfactory compromise. But that works, too.

Brainstorm as many solutions to the problem presented as you can, and then list them on the same piece of paper. Make as many suggestions as you can, even though some of them may not work. Take turns sharing ideas, continuing until you find one that is as close as you can get to a both/and synthesis.

Here are some examples:

"I'll get up early so that I can use the bathroom before you do." Or, "How about buying a double sink?"

"I'll make my telephone calls after nine at night, when you're watching television." Or, "Can you limit the calls to thirty minutes?"

"Why don't you fill the gas tank when it's below quarter full." Or, "Whoever uses the car on Saturday morning can fill the tank."

If you can't find a new synthesis after ten minutes, return to your double vision statements to recall the feelings and the fears that are standing in the way of giving and receiving. Then try again. If you continue to fail, decide on another time when you'll try once more. Sometimes living with a conflict for a while helps to solve it.

Make a record of this work in your journals. Then applaud your capacity to face conflict directly, even if not perfectly.

Exercise Five: Gender Roles and Your Sex Life

Part I. Who Are You?

Because men and women learn to think and act as if they belong to different species, sex is often knotted and snarled by stereotypes and all the judgments implicit in them. In this exercise, you'll loosen the hold of these generalizations. The goal is to feel more authentic, more "you," and that means making sexual choices based on choice and personal desire. Do this exercise sitting together but working separately.

Think of activities traditionally performed well by the other gender that you do well. If you're a woman, you may be able to think rationally, hit a baseball, initiate sex, manage money. If you're a man, you may be able to diaper a baby, take part in an open, intimate conversation, use your intuition, enjoy cuddling and hugging. List these in your journal.

Now choose an activity traditionally performed well by the other gender that you either don't do or do poorly. But this time select a sexual activity. For instance, as a woman you may be unlikely to call for a date, initiate sex, move toward what you want sexually, or initiate a new activity in bed. Or, as a man you may be unlikely to enjoy being romantic, cuddle or hug, share intimate thoughts, or ask for help when you're confused about what to do next. Record what you each have learned in your journals.

Part II. Envisioning a More Authentic "You"

Imagine engaging in the activity you don't do well. Be aware of your felt sense as you do this. Listen to what your inner voice has to say.

Perhaps you feel self-conscious because it's not what your part-ner would want. Or, you feel tight and embarrassed.

Instead of moving away from the activity if it makes you un-comfortable, move toward it in your mind. If you're uncomfort-able or anxious, relax your muscles and wait for the feelings to dissipate.

When you are both finished, share what you have learned.

Then decide if you want to actually experiment with the situa-tions you imagined. If you do, read on. If not, enjoy your freedom to play with different roles in your mind. That, too, is important. Write about what you have learned.

Part III. Using Resonant Intention

Plan for your chosen activities. Decide with your partner when and where you will experiment and who will begin. Since your ac-tivity might bring you into the other person's gender sphere, it's important to ask for your partner's cooperation. For example, if you're choosing to be particularly active during a sexual experi-ence, ask for the other's agreement. If you're choosing to be yield-ing and acquiescent during sex, ask for agreement.

After you have experimented with the change, share your feel-ings and thoughts. Loosening the gender prescriptions during the sexual experience can be an awakening experience. Use your dou-ble vision to understand and empathize.

Set a time for the next exercise.

Exercise Six: Intimate Time

Part I. Creating the Rhythm

The most important gift you and your partner can give each other is the repeated experience of intimate time—those dedicated moments when you are each the other's focus of attention. Only then can you each enjoy the rhythm of pulsing back and forth from your thoughts to his or her thoughts, from your actions to his or her actions. As long as your attention remains focused on each other, intimate time can take place anywhere—walking in a mall, playing in an amusement park, or watching a waterfall. It cannot take place if you have another purpose in mind, whether it be shopping, watching television, or being with friends.

To begin this exercise, simply have a conversation, but as you do, create a rhythm in which each person has time to talk while the other listens. Take turns remembering significant events in your relationship: Recall the moment you met, the first time you were sexual, the day you moved in together. Sense the beat as each person speaks and then listens, speaks and then listens.

When you are finished, talk with your partner about your joint capacity to create this rhythm. If it's difficult, try not to blame each other. This is a two-person problem. Consider, instead, experimenting with other rhythmic activities, like dancing or playing tennis.

To create a rhythm, you need to let go of any self-consciousness and feel yourself as part of a duo, in relation to each other. Then, if you feel your partner respond to your moves, and if you feel yourself respond to his or hers, you're creating an interactive beat even if it's awkward at first. This is the kind of nonverbal work that leads to experiences of resonance.

Part II. Creating a Ritual

A ritual is a repeated set of practices that has symbolic importance. If your loving is complicated by the demands of career or children, you'll find that a well-formed ritual ensures that you have time to connect. I know many couples with children who ask grandparents to babysit so they can devote several weekends a year to their relationship. Others exchange babysitting with friends so that they have privacy in their own homes on a Sunday afternoon every other weekend. Busy, dual-career couples have weekly dinners at quiet restaurants or jog in the park every other morning.

Brainstorm the design for your ritual. Identify a period of time, anywhere from fifteen minutes to several hours. Consider the frequency you prefer, whether it's once a week or once a month. Locate a place, or several places, conducive to intimate time. Record the period of time, the frequency, and the places in your journals.

Use your intention to commit to the ritual. Keep in mind that your ritual will undergo many modifications as you continue your search for resonance.

Finally, recall that the peak experiences of resonance are more likely to occur if you do the following.

> Increase your capacity to focus on your own thoughts and feelings, and use this information to speak with an authentic voice.
>
> Develop your capacity for double vision so that you can maintain your own voice while valuing your partner's voice.
>
> Change dysfunctional patterns, while managing the fears of abandonment and engulfment.
>
> Learn to share power so that neither one of you feels controlled.

Develop your capacity to be angry without being hostile.

Reject gender prescriptions that don't work, and try to make everyday choices based on talent and desire.

Spend more of your life together in intimate time.

Notes

Introduction

The peak experiences of love are important in themselves, but they are also critical to this book because they grant us a fleeting glimpse of the resonant relationship in action. The safety, the creative power, the independence, and the intimacy that characterize the resonant relationship are all present in these moments, if only briefly. Often thrilling, these peak experiences can be frightening—if we're not ready for them.

The metaphor of a jazz group illustrates how resonance is like a flow through time. See Csikszentmihalyi's *Flow* for a review of the psychological research exploring the peak experiences of individuals. They are closely connected but distinct from a couple's peak experiences.

Pages 6–7. Love stories are a product of their times; they reveal what people thought about the moments of abandon and the thrill of connection at different times in history or in different cultures. These stories also tell us about the freedom people had to explore their passion. The love stories reviewed indicate that throughout Western history their freedom was minimal, their fear extreme, and the cost high.

See Robert A. Johnson's *We* for a Jungian view of the Tristram and Isolde myth and the association of woman with "other"; in this case, "the pure, the sacred and the whole." Such a perfect image is bound to fall apart in everyday life, in the end ensuring that passionate love will fail.

Denis de Rougemont's *Love in the Western World* explains why love so often fails in our culture. He argues that the problem began during the Middle Ages when orthodox religion was at war with love. In the antisexual society of that time, people assumed that sex was meant for reproduction only and sexual passion could only be felt outside of marriage. So sexual passion was considered a threat to the family and the social order. In addition, those who believed that religious passion could only be felt directly or mystically, rather than through established creed, were branded as rebels and heretics. This sort of passion was another threat to the church and established society. With this history, passionate love has come to be associated with immoral, sinful behavior.

1 ■ *Vision of Love*

This chapter, and the book as a whole, hinges on the idea that the way we make sense of our lives, how we envision love, profoundly affects the way we shape our everyday lives. There are many ways to shape a vision of love; through faith, myth, philosophy, language, and the social sciences.

See C. S. Lewis' *The Four Loves* for an essay on love and faith.

Joseph Campbell explores the mythic route in *Myths to Live By* in which he speaks to the need people have for a mythology that provides models for being and loving.

Alfred North Whitehead explores the philosophic route. See *Modes of Thought,* p. 63: "The sort of ideas we attend to, and the sort of ideas which we push into the negligible background, govern our hopes, our fears, our control of behavior. As we think, we live."

The sociologist Alfred Schutz suggests that each culture has a range of ideas that make up a "stock of knowledge" transmitted across the generations and used by individuals to "create" their lives. Our institutions, be they schools, governments, or marriages, are made anew by individuals in each generation making use of this "stock of knowledge." This contradicts the all-too-common and disempowering belief that institutions such as marriage are made for us by others and cannot be changed.

Peter Berger and Hansfried Kellner, two sociologists, identify the same reality-building behavior in intimate relationships. See "Marriage and the Construction of Reality," in *Recent Sociology no. 2*, p. 57: "marriage partners are . . . embarked on the often difficult task of constructing for themselves the . . . world in which they will live." These authors suggest that individuals "redefine" themselves in the first phase of a relationship, modifying their understanding of their personal pasts, interpreting their present, and creating dreams of a shared future. As we communicate, we create our relationships.

Roland Barthes's *A Lover's Discourse* looks at love through the multiple meanings embedded in the word itself. It becomes apparent that, without awareness, we shape our relationships according to the value placed on each of these various meanings. As we use words, we live.

Page 19. Alfred Schutz describes what he calls the "interpretive schemes" or "domains of relevance"—what I call the visions through which we make sense of our everyday lives. These visions shift from generation to generation; from urban to suburban to rural cultures; from poor to rich. So, for instance, in our understanding of love, the age it's supposed to happen, how long it's supposed to last, and the kind of loyalty it demands are all part of a vision.

While there are multiple visions of love in any culture, the primary vision, the "ideas in good currency" (see Donald Schon's *Beyond the Stable State*) have changed from merged to exchange over the past forty years. Not that merging has disappeared, it simply isn't as favored as the more modern exchange, particularly if you happen to live in an urban environment.

Resonance is still another vision that is part of our cultural heritage even though it isn't as commonly known. We are guided by those visions as we create our relationships—and the first step toward creating a relationship that works is to access your personal vision.

2 ▪ *The Exchange Relationship*

A major thesis in this book is that there are three cohesive visions of love available to couples in our culture as they shape their relationships: The first vision emphasizes personal freedom rather than togetherness. It leads to a relationship that is an equal exchange between individuals who respect each other's private interests. It's a theory of costs and rewards.

Individuals choose partners or relationship behaviors that offer the greatest reward for the least cost. See "Choice, Exchange, and the Family" by F. Ivan Nye, in *Contemporary Theories About the Family*, as well as Karen S. Cook's *Social Exchange Theory.*

Considerable literature has been written describing the exchange partnership and its problems. For example, see J. Scanzoni's *Sex Roles, Women's Work and Marital Conflict.*

See Phyllis Rose's *Parallel Lives* for the story of Harriet Turner and John Stuart Mill and their late-nineteenth-century attempt at a relationship based on equality. Theirs was a democratic vision of family life, but attempted in a patriarchal era. It was a relationship before its time, so it was met with disbelief, cynicism, and outright anger.

The exchange is a competitive, symmetrical relationship (see *Naven* by Gregory Bateson, and Sluzki and Bevin's "Symmetry and Complementarity" in *The Interactional View*).

3 ▪ *Merging*

A second vision through which we understand loving relationships limits personal freedom and encourages togetherness. It leads to an interactional style described by family therapists; in particular, see Salvador Minuchin's *Families & Family Therapy* (p. 55) for a description of the "enmeshed" family structure with the "heightened sense of belonging (that) requires a major yielding of autonomy." The merged relationship described in this book is similar, but based in a particular historical context—the post–World War II era with socioeconomic and political forces that fostered this suburban, insulated, and patriarchal form of relationship. Placing relationships in the context of history makes clear how the shifting nature of culture—the zeitgeist or the spirit of the times—emphasizes or de-emphasizes the "I" or the "we."

Merging is a complementary relationship (see Bateson's *Naven* and Sluzki and Bevin's *Symmetry and Complementarity*).

4 ▪ *Resonance*

The tradition in which resonant relationships emerge is not dominant in our culture; however, it does exist, and it is followed by those on a humanistic or spiritual path. Their focus is on the value of each person and the web of meanings that is established between people. See Gregory Bateson's *Mind and Nature,* in which he proposes that "mind," or the thinking process, isn't internal to the individual but exists in the range of meanings that link people together. He acknowledges the existence of a larger whole, the "we," as people communicate.

I am indebted to Martin Buber's *The Knowledge of Man* and *I and Thou.* This existential philosopher describes the I-thou relationship as a dialogue that assumes, and therefore calls forth, God in each person. His is a philosophy of the "inter-human" or the "in-between" rather than of the individual or of isolated individuals in a mass society. It is about that which takes place *between* individuals who are *unique* and striving to see each other in the clarity of the present moment. The I-thou relationship is one of deeply felt mutual respect. Each individual is a spirit-filled subject rather than an impersonal object.

Jurgen Habermas (see "Toward a Theory of Communicative Competence" in *Recent Sociology)* also distinguishes the realm of the "we" from the realm of the "I," calling the former "intersubjective." Habermas suggests that there are linguistic rules embedded in culture that make the intersubjective possible. If followed, these linguistic rules lead to "communication competence," which means that, first, people search for a consensus in regard to "truth." They understand that there is a difference between subjective feelings and group-held interpretations of reality. Second, they communicate so as to maintain each individual's freedom, selecting information to reveal and information to keep private. Finally, they communicate in the realm of justice—"shoulds," which are judgments of actions and intentions. Such a dialogue fosters truth, freedom, and justice.

I am indebted to Alfred Roberts for his work on *Reciprocal Resonance,* and the perception that the capacity for this rhythm is built into the physiology of human beings and functions so as to link us together.

Mihaly Csikszenthmihalyi's *Flow* is the research psychologist's contribution to an understanding of the peak experiences of life, some of which occur in relationships. This research indicates findings similar to some of those I have found in my clinical work. According to Csikszenthmihaly, peak experiences are characterized by the ability to focus intensely on a part of life, deep but effortless awareness, an absence of concern for the self, time that loses meaning. My findings indicate that for couples they are also characterized by a sense of safety, creative rather than control power, an absence of strict gender prescriptions, and the capacity to create an interactive beat.

Page 74. See William Blake's "Gnomic Verses."

Pages 74–75. See *Song of Songs: A New Translation,* translated by Marcia Falk. San Francisco: HarperSanFrancisco, 1990.

Pages 75–76. See D. H. Lawrence's "Love Was Once a Little Boy," in *Phoenix II: Uncollected, Unpublished and Other Prose Works.*

Page 76. See Martin Buber's *I and Thou.*

5 ▪ *The Tools of Resonance*

This chapter introduces two other themes that are woven into this book. The first is that we can understand ourselves in relation to the patterns we follow. These patterns are built into the systems (families, cultures, or the larger wholes) within which we live. The second is that there are tools that can be used to undo these patterns.

Pages 89–92. See Gregory Bateson's *Steps to an Ecology of Mind* and *Mind and Nature* for the early work on pattern through time. See Lynn Hoffman's *Foundations of Family Therapy* for her analysis of pattern in families. Finally, see James Gleick's *Chaos* for a view of how pattern is built into the most complex of natural phenomena—reoccurring with some frequency, but never fully predictable.

See Boszormenyi-Nagy and Spark's *Invisible Loyalties* for a look at the multigenerational family, with its patterns across long periods of time.

Pages 92–95. Our world consists of wholes that fit together so they are all of a piece. When we are aware of some of the rules that govern this complicated set of contexts we have a chance to shape those rules to suit our needs. The discovery of such rules was given modern form by the early anthropologists who studied culture as context. See Margaret Mead's *Continuities in Cultural Evolution* and Ruth Benedict's *Patterns of Culture.*

In *Design for Evolution,* Erich Jantsch explores human systems and the tendency people have to think in either/or polarities such as right/wrong, nature/culture, individual/community. He suggests that there is a need to live out the tension between these opposites to allow for a fluidity that leads toward change. He explores the regulating principles that shape living systems—the culturewide patterns that we live.

See Arthur Koestler's *Janus* for his suggestion that human beings have a two-sided nature, and this underlies the tendency toward polarized (either/or) patterns: There is the part of us that looks inward and is self-concerned and the part of us that looks outward and is other-concerned. Therefore, human nature is both self-assertive (a function of the human being's separate physiology), and integrative ("manifested in flexible strategies and creative syntheses"). The independence/intimacy polarity, he says, is therefore built into the human experience.

Analysis of polarized patterns indicates two types: complementary and symmetrical. See Gregory Bateson's *Naven*, and Sluzki and Bevin's "Symmetry and Complementarity," in *The Interactional View.* In complementary interactions more of a certain behavior on A's part results in more of a different but complementary behavior on B's part. The behaviors mutually fit; for example, the more one person is dominant, the more the other is submissive. In symmetrical interactions, people are equals and exchange the same behaviors. If A works, B works; if A spends money, B spends money. Both set the rules for their relationship. In this book, I argue that people who merge tend toward *complementary* interactions while people in an exchange tend toward *symmetrical* interactions. Each of the polarized patterns described in this chapter can take complementary or symmetrical forms.

There is, however, a third form of interaction, the *both/and* interaction, in which a behavior on A's part leads to a *differentiated* behavior on B's part. Each person recognizes both sides of the polarity within themselves, then reacts based on personal need and perception of the other's need.

Pages 95–100. Of the resonant skills, the ability to focus inside oneself is essential. This skill is developed in therapy, in prayer, in art forms, and in various forms of meditation. Freud, of course, led the way for Western psychology (*New Introductory Lectures on Psychoanalysis*). Also see the psychologist Eugene T. Gendlin's *Focusing*—the conceptualization of the "felt sense" as a psychological tool was developed by him. Goldstein and Kornfield's *Seeking The Heart of Wisdom* is a description of ancient Buddhist approach to focusing called "insight" or "vipassana" meditation. See Feldenkrais's *Awareness Through Movement* for the approach to self-knowledge that comes through focusing on bodily action.

Pages 101–104. A second important skill is the ability to use double vision—a skill that is grounded in both the self-assertive and integrative sides of the human being. For a close approximation to the double vision tool, see Martin Buber's "Distance and relation" in *The Knowledge of Man*. Pages 62–63 of this book include an analysis of the new synthesis that occurs when two people perceive themselves to be part of a larger whole. Paying attention to the union, or to the fabric that connects them, couples are more likely to value it and so keep it intact. This oscillating shift in attention from oneself to the other and the larger whole is necessary for the resonant union.

Pages 104–107. Resonant intention depends on the cultivation of the will. See Roberto Assagioli's *Psychosynthesis* and Rollo May's *Love and Will*.

6 ▪ *Power and Control*

Understanding our cultural "take" on power, and the effect this has on our lives, is important because it can lead to the creation of a perceptual boundary that allows us to screen out these assumptions and makes room for a resonant approach to power.

The attempt to dominate is a problem in many arenas of our lives. For example, see Philippe Aries's *Centuries of Childhood* for an accounting of the mistreatment of children, Michel Foucault's *Madness & Civilization* for an analysis of the abuse of the mentally ill, and finally, Thomas Kuhn's "The Structure of Scientific Revolutions" in the *International Encyclopedia of Unified Science* for a view of how established scientists silence those with differing views. In his time, Marx crystallized the abuse of working people in *The German Ideology,* and in the last several decades many feminists have done the same regarding the abuse of women. For example, see Lillian Rubin's *Worlds of Pain*.

Pages 110–112. I am indebted to Elizabeth Janeway and her book, *Powers of the Weak,* for her analysis of overt and covert power. The blind spots of the merged power system are apparent once we see that the so-called powerful person is being fought by the so-called powerless person, often very effectively.

See Gene Sharp's *The Politics of Nonviolent Action* for a political analysis of the fragility of relationships built on force, and for a review of nonviolent power.

Pages 118–119. See Kenneth E. Boulding's *Three Faces of Power* for a breakdown of the forms of power that approximates the categories used in this chapter. Defining power as a potential for change, he identifies (1) threat power, a destructive form akin to merged power; (2) economic power, a form that rests on the capacity to exchange items; and (3) integrative power, found in relationships that include respect, affection, and love. An economist by training, Boulding describes how these forms of power play their part in our institutions.

7 ▪ *Anger Yes, Hostility No*

In our culture, preoccupation with individuality and a blindness to the unions, or the networks of meanings, that connect us has led to a widespread indulgence in impulsive hostility. This indulgence tears holes in the connective tissue that holds us together. Unfortunately, many people believe that the free expression of hostility is healthy. See Theodore Rubin's *The Angry Book*, in which there is a focus on the "I" and little awareness of the "we."

Pages 127–130. See Harriet G. Lerner's *The Dance of Anger* to learn about feeling the strength that comes of maintaining a separate voice. Following the psychotherapist Murray Bowen, however, she pays little attention to furthering the development of the union, even through anger.

Also see Polly Young-Eisendrath and Florence Wiedemann's *Female Authority*. This is a book that grows out of the Jungian and feminist traditions. While Jung, through his introduction of the "collective unconscious," contributed much to our awareness of the network of meanings that connects us, this book is primarily focused on the "I."

David Mace, in *Love and Anger in Marriage*, pages 106–108, develops a practical approach to anger in which two people use the written word to identify each person's perspective and then correct the other's statement in an effort to develop what, in this book, is called double vision. This moves closer to the idea that resolutions can go beyond each person's perspective and ultimately become a shared perspective.

Pages 138–144. See Alan Parry's "A Universe of Stories" in the journal *Family Process* for the postmodern view that each life is a story, and that we are characters in each other's stories. Out of this approach comes the idea that we can only transcend "the limitation of our own vantage points through imagination and curiosity." See Jose Ortega y Gasset's *On Love* for his conviction that it is the human capacity for curiosity that leads to an understanding of the other that goes beyond the self. This is the kind of thinking that leads to using anger well in relationships.

8 ▪ *The Gender Trap*

The focus of this chapter is on the human being's tendency to create hierarchies of better or worse people, and our capacity to transcend that thinking. Hierarchical thinking underlies the gender problem. See Riane Eisler's *The Chalice and the Blade* for what she calls the dominator model (what is popularly called either patriarchy or matriarchy—the ranking of one-half of humanity over the other that is based on force.) She compares this with a partnership model, which is based on the principle of linking rather than ranking. It's a both/and model for gender relationships. The book reviews archaeological studies that indicate a prehistoric and regressive shift from the pastoral, more "equalitarian," society to the current patriarchy.

Pages 147–149. See Aafke Komter's study, "Hidden Power in Marriage" in *Gender & Society*, which offers an analysis of what she calls "hidden power," the implicit values and beliefs that precede and guide behavior and are not touched by rational thought or experience. These explanations for behavior take the form of stereotypes. For instance, the perceptions that women like homemaking more than men, or that men are born to lead, are maintained even when reason or a person's actual experience contradicts them.

Abstractions, whether they be hierarchies of worth or gender stereotypes, interfere with the immediacy of resonance. See Maurice Friedman's "The Basis of Buber's Ethics" in *The Philosophy of Martin Buber* for a description of the concreteness of the I-thou experience, and the recognition that abstractions interfere with the unique, in-the-moment, relationship between two people.

Page 149. See Plato in *The Works of Plato* for the tale of his original beings who were whole, and then were split in half by Zeus in punishment.

Pages 149–155. See John Stuart Mill's *The Subjection of Women* for his views about the treatment of women during the middle of the nineteenth century. See Jessie Bernard's *The Female World* for an analysis of the social learning that separates men and women into two markedly different cultural groups. See Carol Gilligan's *In a Different Voice* for a view of how the "female" culture is alive and different, but submerged in the male culture. Finally, see Deborah Tannen's *You Just Don't Understand* for a sociolinguistic analysis of the differences in male and female speech patterns, and how that interferes with human connection.

Patriarchal gender norms are built into family life. They are also built into the work of Freud (see Nancy Chodorow's *Feminism and Psychoanalytic Theory,*) and into psychological theories of family life (see Rachel Hare-Mustin's "The Problem of Gender in Family Therapy Theory" in *Family Process*). See Jessica Benjamin's *Bonds of Love* for a feminist analysis of the gender role formulas built into psychological theories which make it likely that a woman will not be seen as healthy.

Pages 155–156. I am indebted to Alyson Scott for her use of the rainbow metaphor to describe the range of human characteristics we usually put into two dichotomous groups—male and female.

Pages 156–165. Gender norms are also built into age-old myths, (see Jean Shinoda Bolen's *Goddesses in Every Woman*). Often, these descriptions become *pre*scriptions for people searching for guidance *outside themselves* regarding the relationship between the genders. My suggestion is to go to these myths only to understand how female identities have been viewed over time, and then to explore one's own interests and talents to develop as a human being. See Carolyn Heilbrun's *Toward a Recognition of Androgyny* for a search into myth and literature for manifestations of a human nature beyond gender roles.

See Claremont de Castillejo's *Knowing Woman: A Feminine Psychology* for a discussion of the engulfment/abandonment polarity and its connection to the male/female polarity. See Carol Gilligan's *In a Different Voice* for the suggestion that the integrative aspect of the human being is reflective of "an ethic of caring."

9 ▪ *Feeling the Beat*

See chapter five of Edward Hall's *Beyond Culture* for a description of research being done on the rhythm that two people develop when they're close. Also see Ray Birdwhistell's *Kinesics and Context* and a report on the work of Frederick Erickson at the University of Pennsylvania in *Psychology Today* for further work on interactive rhythm.

See Rebecca Warner's "Rhythm in Social Interaction" in *The Social Psychology of Time* for a review of major research on the effect of being in or out of rhythm in close relationships.

Pages 169–172. Read *Alfred Schutz On Phenomenology and Social Relations*, chapter 12, for an analysis of the discrete "provinces of meaning" we live within, and how time itself is experienced differently within each one. For example, everyday life, fantasy, art, religious experience, and scientific research each have their own experience of time. Similarly, intimacy offers a discrete experience of time.

For a review of the various kinds of time we live by, see Edward Hall's *The Dance of Life.*

In *Inside the Family*, David Kantor and William Lehr suggest that time itself is a dimension of family life, and that it changes given different types of families.

Pages 172–176. See a study of "morning and night couples" by Larson, Crane, and Smith. Couples whose awake and sleep patterns are mismatched (e.g. a person who gets up early in the morning and goes to sleep early in the evening married to a person who gets up late in the morning and goes to sleep late in the evening) score lower on marital adjustment scales than couples who are matched. Mismatched but happy couples had greater flexibility when managing conflict.

Pages 176–177. For an understanding of "now" time, see Eugen Herrigel's *Zen in the Art of Archery,* a description of the zen discipline that leads toward the experience of timelessness. Also, *Japanese Haiku*, translated by Peter Beilenson—a form of poetry devoted to expressing the now experience.

Page 179. See Werner et al., "Temporal Qualities of Rituals and Celebrations" in *The Social Psychology of Time* for a description of how scale, rhythm, pace, and sequencing come together to make an event significant.

10 ▪ *Resonant Sex*

The sexual context is ripe for experiences of resonance. The problem is, however, that many couples follow sexual patterns that make resonance impossible. But the good news is that because sex is a cutting edge in many relationship, changing these sexual patterns can lead to a resonant relationship. For a review of our thinking about sexuality, see William H. Masters and Virginia E. Johnson's *Human Sexual Response.* Also, see Maggie Scarf's *Intimate Partners.* Shere Hite's *Women and Love* offers a view of the beliefs women hold about sex.

Pages 186–191. See Pauline Reage's *The Story of O* for a powerful depiction of master/slave sexuality, a fantasy that came from the mind of a woman. It describes the reciprocity of this particular kind of relationship.

For a description of a psychoanalytic approach to dominance and sexual control, see Jessica Benjamin's *Bonds of Love*. Beginning with a definition of power as control over another person, and concurring with Freud that domination is inevitable, she traces male domination of women back to early development. She suggests that males "objectify" their mothers (see them more like things than human beings) in order to separate. Thereafter men are "subjects" while women remain "objects." More important for this book, however, as a feminist she also recognizes that there are other determinants of behavior besides early development; for instance, the social learning that polarizes the genders and deprives both males and females of an opportunity to know each other as two subjects. She concludes that if two people can be subjects to each other, they can have a relationship in which one person's assertion receives a "recognizing response"—a respectful reaction—from the other. In this way, she moves toward the mutuality that I argue is not only possible but essential to sexual resonance.

Pages 193–200. For a description of passion that approaches the rhythmicity of resonance, see Ethel Spector Person's *Dreams of Love and Fateful Encounters*.

Also see John Welwood's compilation of literary reflections on love, sex, and intimacy in *Challenge of the Heart*. In particular, an excerpt from the philosopher Ortega y Gasset's *On Love* emphasizes the lover's need for a special kind of understanding, one that includes a full sense of the loved one as a separate human being. D. H. Lawrence's "The Stream of Desire" is a metaphor for the "I" and the "we" of resonant sexuality.

11 ▪ *The Money Tool*

This chapter argues that money is a tool that can be used to enhance or destroy relationships. See the introduction to *Georg Simmel: On Women, Sexuality, and Love* by Guy Oakes for an analysis of how the measuring tool called money can destroy the value of that which it measures. According to Simmel, our modern society exhibits an increasingly large range of "cultural artifacts" that hold value, and that becomes confusing to people. It's too much. Money is an instrument that, first, is a uniform scale for measurement, and so tends to standardize anything it measures. For instance, sixteenth-century paintings and late-twentieth-century TV performances are measured on the same financial scale. With things thus standardized, we can ask how much money does each cost, and believe this is the only measure of "value." Second, money is an instrument with only one characteristic, the capacity to measure quantity, so it is an interchangeable artifact. Without other qualities, it can be used in place of other artifacts. It therefore becomes "the value by which the worth of every other artifact is defined." And that leads to the destruction of other kinds of values—the quality of an artist's work or even the experience of an afternoon spent walking in the woods. Perhaps most important, when we use money to value things, we move further and further away from the immediacy of experience, and we feel less related to the process of creating them.

Pages 216–218. See Barbara Fishman's "The Economic Behavior of Stepfamilies" in *Family Relations* for a descriptions of the more traditional "one-pot," the exchange "two-pot" families, and those who create "three pots"—one for each partner and one for the union. Families in this last group create the flexible financial structure that allows for personal freedom as well as closeness.

Bibliography

Aries, Philippe. *Centuries of Childhood*. New York: Vintage Books, 1965.

Assagioli, Roberto. *Psychosynthesis*. New York: Hobbs, Dorman & Co., 1965

Barthes, Roland. *A Lover's Discourse*. Translated by Richard Howard. New York: Hill and Wang, 1978.

Bateson, Gregory. *Steps to an Ecology of Mind*. New York: Chandler Publishing Co., 1972.

———. *Naven*. 2d ed. Stanford: Stanford Univ. Press, 1958.

———. *Mind and Nature: A Necessary Unity*. New York: E. P. Dutton, 1979.

Benedict, Ruth. *Patterns of Culture*. New York: Houghton Mifflin, 1946.

Benjamin, Jessica. *Bonds of Love*. New York: Random House, 1988.

Bepko, Claudia, with Jo Ann Krestan. *The Responsibility Trap: A Blueprint for Treating the Alcoholic Family*. New York: Free Press, 1985.

Berger, Peter, and Hansfried Kellner. "Marriage and the Construction of Reality." In *Recent Sociology no. 2.* Edited by Hans Peter Dreitzel. New York: Macmillan, 1970.

———, and Thomas Luckmann. *The Social Construction of Reality.* New York: Doubleday/Anchor, 1966.

Bernard, Jessie. *The Female World.* New York: Free Press, 1981.

Birdwhistell, Ray L. *Kinesics and Context.* Philadelphia: Univ. of Pennsylvania Press, 1970.

Blake, William. "Gnomic Verses." In *Selected Poems by William Blake,* introduction by Basil de Sélincourt. London: Oxford Univ. Press, 1951.

Bolen, Jean Shinoda. *Goddesses in Every Woman.* New York: Harper & Row, 1984.

Boszormenyi-Nagy, Ivan, and Geraldine M. Spark. *Invisible Loyalties.* New York: Harper & Row, 1973.

Boulding, Kenneth E. *Three Faces of Power.* Newbury Park, CA: Sage Publications, 1989.

Bowlby, John. *Attachment.* New York: Basic Books, 1969.

Buber, Martin. *Between Man and Man.* Translated by Ronald Gregor Smith. New York: Macmillan, 1947.

———. *The Knowledge of Man: A Philosophy of the Interhuman.* Translated by Maurice Friedman. New York: Harper & Row, 1965.

———. *I and Thou.* Translated by Walter Kaufmann. New York: Charles Scribner's Sons, 1970.

Burr, W., R. Wesley, Reuben Hill, F. Ivan Nye, and Ira Reiss, eds. *Contemporary Theories About the Family.* Vol. 2 New York: Free Press, 1979.

Campbell, Joseph. *Hero with a Thousand Faces.* Princeton: Princeton Univ. Press, 1949.

———. *Myths to Live By.* New York: Viking Press, 1972.

Carter, Elizabeth A., and Monica McGoldrick. *The Family Life Cycle: A Framework for Family Therapy.* New York: Gardner Press, Inc., 1980.

Castillejo, Claremont de. *Knowing Woman: A Feminine Psychology.* New York: Harper & Row, 1973.

Chasin, Richard, Sallyann Roth, and Michele Bogard. "Action Methods in Systemic Therapy." *Family Process* 28, no. 2 (June 1989): 121–136.

Chodorow, Nancy. *Feminism and Psychoanalytic Theory.* New Haven: Yale Univ. Press, 1989.

Combrick-Graham, Lee. "A Developmental Model for Family Systems." *Family Process* 24, no. 2 (June 1985): 139–150.

Connerton, Paul, ed. *Critical Sociology.* New York: Penguin Books, 1976.

Cook, Karen S., ed. *Social Exchange Theory.* Newbury Park, CA: Sage Publications, 1987.

Csikszenthmihalyi, Mihaly. *Flow: The Psychology of Optimal Experience.* New York: Harper & Row, 1990.

Edlund, Matthew. *Psychological Time and Mental Illness.* New York: Gardner Press, Inc., 1987.

Eisler, Riane. *The Chalice and the Blade.* San Francisco: Harper & Row, 1987.

Elkaim, Mony. "A Systemic Approach to Couple Therapy." *Family Process* 25, no. 1 (March 1986): 35–42.

Erikson, Erik H. *Identity and the Life Cycle.* New York: W. W. Norton, 1980.

Erickson, Frederick. Quoted in "The Beat Goes On" by Carole Douglis. *Psychology Today* (November 1987): 37–42.

Falk, Marcia. *Song of Songs: A New Translation.* San Francisco: HarperSanFrancisco, 1990.

Feldenkrais, Moshe. *Awareness Through Movement.* San Francisco: HarperSanFrancisco, 1990.

Fishman, Barbara. "The Economic Behavior of Stepfamilies." *Family Relations* 32 (1983): 359–366.

———, and Robert Fishman. "Enriching Marriage as a Reciprocally Resonant Relationship." In *Prevention in Family Services: Approaches to Family Wellness.* Edited by David Mace. Newbury Park, CA: Sage Publications, 1983.

Foucault, Michel. *The History of Sexuality.* Vol. 1. New York: Vintage Books, 1978.

———. *Madness & Civilization.* New York: Vintage Books, 1973.

Frankl, Victor E. *Man's Search for Meaning.* New York: Washington Square Press, 1985.

Freud, Sigmund. *New Introductory Lectures on Psychoanalysis.* Translated and edited by James Strachey. New York: W. W. Norton, 1965.

Friedman, Maurice. "The Basis of Buber's Ethics." In *The Philosophy of Martin Buber*. Edited by Paul Arthur Schilpp and Maurice Friedman. La Salle, IL: Univ. of Illinois Press, 1967.

Fromm, Erich. *To Have or To Be*. New York: Harper & Row, 1976.

Gendlin, Eugene T. *Focusing*. New York: Bantam Books, 1981.

Gilligan, Carol. *In a Different Voice*. Cambridge, MA: Harvard Univ. Press, 1982.

Gleick, James. *Chaos*. New York: Penguin, 1987.

Goethe, Johann Wolfgang. *The Sorrows of Young Werther*. Translated by Catherine Hunter. New York: The New American Library of World Literature, 1962.

Goldstein, Joseph, and Jack Kornfield. *Seeking the Heart of Wisdom: The Path of Insight Meditation*. Boston: Shambhala Publications, 1987.

Gordon, Thomas. *Parent Effectiveness Training*. New York: P. H. Wyden, 1970.

Habermas, Jürgen. "Toward a Theory of Communicative Competence." In *Recent Sociology no. 2*. Edited by Hans Peter Dreitzel. New York: Macmillan, 1970.

Hall, Edward. *Beyond Culture*. Garden City, NY: Anchor Press/Doubleday, 1976.

———. *The Dance of Life*. Garden City, NY: Anchor Press/Doubleday, 1983.

Hare-Mustin, Rachel T. "The Problem of Gender in Family Therapy Theory." *Family Process* 26, no. 1 (March 1987): 15–28.

Heilbrun, Carolyn G. *Toward a Recognition of Androgyny*. New York: W. W. Norton, 1964.

———. *Writing a Woman's Life*. New York: W. W. Norton, 1988.

Herrigel, Eugen. *Zen in the Art of Archery*. New York: Vintage Books, 1971.

Hite, Shere. *Women and Love: A Cultural Revolution in Progress*. New York: Knopf, 1987.

Hoffman, Lynn. *Foundations of Family Therapy*. New York: Basic Books, 1981.

Janeway, Elizabeth. *Powers of the Weak*. New York: Alfred A. Knopf, 1980.

Japanese Haiku. Translated by Peter Beilenson. Mount Vernon, NY: Peter Pauper Press, 1955.

Jantsch, Erich. *Design for Evolution.* New York: George Braziller, 1975.

Johnson, Robert A. *We: Understanding the Psychology of Romantic Love.* San Francisco: Harper & Row, 1983.

———. *Inner Work: Using Dreams & Active Imagination for Personal Growth.* San Francisco: Harper & Row, 1986.

Joyce, James, *Finnegan's Wake.* New York: Viking Press. 1939.

———. *Ulysses.* New York: Random House, 1986.

Jung, Carl G. *Modern Man in Search of a Soul.* New York: Harcourt, Brace & World, 1933.

Kantor, David, and William Lehr. *Inside the Family.* New York: Harper & Row, 1975.

Koestler, Arthur. *Janus.* New York: Vintage Books, 1978.

Komter, Aafke. "Hidden Power in Marriage." *Gender & Society* 3, no. 2 (June 1989): 187–216.

Kuhn, Thomas. "The Structure of Scientific Revolutions." In *International Encyclopedia of Unified Science.* Vol. 2, no. 2. Chicago: Univ. of Chicago Press, 1962.

Larson, Jeffry H., Russel Crane, and Craig W. Smith. "Morning and Night Couples: The Effect of Wake and Sleep Patterns on Marital Adjustment." *Journal of Marriage and Family Therapy* 17, no. 1 (1991): 53–66.

Lawrence, D. H. *Phoenix II: Uncollected, Unpublished and Other Prose Works.* Edited by Warren Roberts and Harry T. Moore. New York: Viking, 1970.

Lerner, Harriet G. *The Dance of Anger.* New York: Harper & Row, 1985.

Lewis, C. S. *The Four Loves.* New York: Harcourt Brace Jovanovich, 1960.

Mace, David. *Love and Anger in Marriage.* Grand Rapids, MI: Zondervan, 1982.

Marx, Karl, and Frederick Engels. *The German Ideology.* Part I. Edited by C. J. Arthur. New York: International Publishers, 1970.

Maslow, Abraham. *Motivation and Personality.* 2d ed. New York: Harper & Row, 1954.

———. *Toward a Psychology of Being.* 2d ed. New York: Litton Educational Publishing, 1968.

Masters, William H., and Virginia E. Johnson. *Human Sexual Response.* Boston: Little, Brown & Co., 1966.

May, Rollo. *Love and Will.* New York: W. W. Norton, 1969.

McGrath, Joseph E., ed. *The Social Psychology of Time: New Perspectives.* Newbury Park, CA: Sage Publications, 1988.

Melito, Richard. "Adaptation in Family Systems: A Developmental Perspective." *Family Process* 24, no. 3 (September 1985): 89–100.

Mead, Margaret. *Continuities in Cultural Evolution.* New Haven, CT: Yale Univ. Press, 1964

Mill, John Stuart. *The Subjection of Women.* Cambridge, MA: MIT Press, 1989.

Mills, C. Wright. *The Sociological Imagination.* New York: Oxford Univ. Press, 1959.

Minuchin, Salvador. *Families & Family Therapy.* Cambridge, MA: Harvard Univ. Press, 1974.

Nye, F. Ivan. "Choice, Exchange, and the Family." In *Contemporary Theories About the Family.* Vol. 2. Edited by W. Burr, R. Wesley, Reuben Hill, F. Ivan Nye, and Ira Reiss. New York: Free Press, 1979.

Ortega y Gasset, Jose. *On Love.* Translated by Tony Talbot. New York: Meridian Books, 1957.

Parry, Alan. "A Universe of Stories." *Family Process* 30, no. 1 (1991): 37–54.

Person, Ethel Spector. *Dreams of Love and Fateful Encounters: The Power of Romantic Passion.* New York: W. W. Norton, 1988.

Plato. *The Works of Plato.* Edited by Irwin Edman. New York: Simon & Schuster, 1928.

Roberts, Alfred. *Rhythmical Patterning in Human Behavior.* Unpublished paper.

Reage, Pauline. *Story of O.* Translated by Sabine d'Estree. New York: Grove Press, 1965.

Rose, Phyllis. *Parallel Lives: Five Victorian Marriages.* New York: Alfred Knopf, 1983.

Rougemont, Denis de. *Love in the Western World.* Translated by Montgomery Belgion. New York: Harcourt, Brace, 1940.

Rubin, Lillian. *Worlds of Pain.* New York: Basic Books, 1976.

Rubin, Theodore Isaac. *The Angry Book.* New York: Collier, 1970.

Scanzoni, John. *Sex Roles, Women's Work and Marital Conflict.* Lexington, MA: D.C. Heath, 1979.

Scarf, Maggie. *Intimate Partners: Patterns in Love and Marriage.* New York: Ballantine Books, 1987.

Schon, Donald A. *Beyond the Stable State.* New York: W. W. Norton, 1971.

Schutz, Alfred. *Alfred Schutz: On Phenomenology and Social Relations.* Edited by Helmut R. Wagner. Chicago: Univ. of Chicago Press, 1970.

Sharp, Gene. *The Politics of Nonviolent Action. Part One: Power and Struggle.* Boston: Porter Sargent Publishers, 1973.

Simmel, Georg. *George Simmel: On Women, Sexuality, and Love.* Translated by Guy Oakes. New Haven, CT: Yale Univ. Press, 1984.

Sluzki, C., and J. Bevin. "Symmetry and Complementarity: An Operational Definition and a Typology of Dyads." In *The Interactional View.* Edited by Paul Watzlawick and J. Weakland. New York: W. W. Norton, 1977.

Spitze, Glenna. "Women's Employment and Family Relations." *Journal of Marriage and the Family* 50, no. 3 (August 1988): 595–618.

Stendhal, Marie-Henri Beyle. *On Love.* New York: W. W. Norton, 1947.

Suzuki, D. T., and Richard De Martino. *Zen Buddhism & Psychoanalysis.* New York: Harper & Row, 1960.

Tannen, Deborah. *You Just Don't Understand: Women and Men in Conversation.* New York: Ballantine Books, 1990.

Taylor, Shelley E. *Positive Illusions.* New York: Basic Books, 1989.

Valliant, George. *Adaption to Life.* Boston: Little, Brown & Co., 1977.

Viorst, Judith. *Necessary Losses.* New York: Simon & Schuster, 1986.

Warner, Rebecca. "Rhythm in Social Interaction." In *The Social Psychology of Time.* Edited by Joseph E. McGrath. Newbury Park, CA: Sage Publications, 1988.

Watzlawick, Paul, John, Weakland, and Richard Fisch. *Change.* New York: W. W. Norton, 1974.

Weitz, Shirley, ed. *Nonverbal Communication.* Oxford, England: Oxford Univ. Press. 1974.

Welwood, John, ed. *Awakening the Heart: East/West Approaches to Psychotherapy and the Healing Relationship.* Boston: Shambhala Publications, 1983.

———. *Challenge of the Heart: Love, Sex and Intimacy in Changing Times.* Boston: Shambhala Publications, 1985.

Werner, Carol M., Lois M. Haggard, Irwin Altman, and Diana Oxley. "Temporal Qualities of Rituals and Celebrations." In *The Social Psychology of Time.* Edited by Joseph E. McGrath. Newbury Park, CA: Sage Publications, 1988.

Whisman, Mark A., and Neil S. Jacobson. "Depression, Marital Satisfaction, and Marital and Personality Measures of Sex Roles." *Journal of Marital and Family Therapy* 15, no. 2 (1989): 177–186.

White, Barbara B. "Gender Differences in Marital Communication Patterns." *Family Process* 28, no. 1 (March 1989): 86–106.

Whitehead, Alfred North. *Modes of Thought.* New York: Macmillan, 1938.

Wiley, M. G., and D. E. Wooley. "Interruptions Among Equals." *Gender and Society* 2, no. 1 (1988): 90–102.

Young-Eisendrath, Polly, and Florence Wiedemann. *Female Authority: Empowering Women Through Psychotherapy.* New York: Guilford Press, 1987.

ACKNOWLEDGMENTS

Grateful acknowledgment is made to Penguin USA for permission to quote from *Phoenix II* by D. H. Lawrence.

Excerpt from "Eighteen Days Without You," *Love Poems,* by Anne Sexton. Copyright © 1967, 1968, 1969 by Anne Sexton. Reprinted by permission of Houghton Mifflin Company. All rights reserved.

Lines from "now all the fingers of this tree (darling) have" are reprinted from *Complete Poems, 1904–1962,* by e. e. cummings, edited by George J. Firmage, by permission of Liveright Publishing Corporation. Copyright © 1949, 1977, 1991 by the Trustees for the E. E. Cummings Trust.

Excerpt from *The Song of Songs: A New Translation and Interpretation* by Marcia Falk. Copyright © 1973, 1977, 1982, 1990 by Marcia Lee Falk. Illustrations copyright © 1990 by Pennyroyal Press. Reprinted by permission of HarperCollins Publishers, Inc.

This book is part of an ongoing effort to explore the nature of resonance and to encourage others to search for it in their own relationships. I would like to hear from you if you want to share your experiences in search of resonance, or if you would like to explore other materials that are available.

Dr. Barbara Miller Fishman
P.O. Box 761
Bala Cynwyd, Pennsylvania 19004
800-666-6306